B08 815 1332 MSC

SCHOOLS LIBRARY SERVICE
Maltby Library Headquarters
High Street
Maltby   MAR 1999
Rotherham S66 8LA

ROTHERHAM PUBLIC LIBRARIES

This book must be returned by the date specified at the time of
issue as the Date Due for Return.
The loan may be extended (personally, by post or telephone) for
a further period, if the book is not required by another reader,
by quoting the above number   LM1 (C)

HAMLYN

HOMER'S ODYSSEY

Homer's Odyssey

RETOLD BY JAROSLAV HULÁK
ILLUSTRATED BY JIŘÍ BĚHOUNEK

HAMLYN

ROTHERHAM LIBRARY &
INFORMATION SERVICES

J883 · 01 HOM
8151332
GIFT

SCHOOLS STOCK

First published 1989
Designed and produced by Artia for
The Hamlyn Publishing Group Limited
Michelin House, 81 Fulham Road,
London SW3 6RB
© Artia, Prague 1988
© This edition by
The Hamlyn Publishing Group Limited 1989
Translated by Stephen Finn
Graphic design by Ivan Urbánek

All rights reserved.
No part of this publication may be reproduced,
stored in a retrieval system, or transmitted,
in any form or by any means, electronic, mechanical,
photocopying, recording, or otherwise,
without the prior permission
of The Hamlyn Publishing Group Limited
and the copyright holders.

ISBN 0 600 56322 7

Printed in Czechoslovakia by Svoboda, Prague
1/23/01/51—01

CONTENTS

REVENGE

Odysseus
and
the Trojan War

Long ago the mighty King Priam ruled over the city of Troy, on the shores of Asia Minor. He and his wife Hecabe lived with their many sons and daughters in the fortress of Pergamon, which towered high above the city walls. Just before the birth of Priam's fiftieth son, the queen had a strange dream: as she took the newborn child in her arms to nurse him, he turned into a blazing firebrand. The flames set fire to the palace, and a great inferno reduced the whole city to ashes. When he heard of this dream, the king sent for the soothsayers to explain its meaning. Their verdict was clear: the son who was to be born to Priam and Hecabe would bring about the destruction of the entire city.

The distraught parents did not know what they should do, but in the end they agreed to leave the boy out on the mountainside to the mercy of the wild beasts. Let him die, rather than bring suffering, pain and death to so many! Let him depart this world, sooner than cause the fall of the whole realm!

Everyone was sure that the baby would die out there in the wilderness, but they were wrong. He was found on the slopes of Mount Ida by an old, childless herdsman, who took the boy home with him and cared for him as his own son. By and by the royal child grew into a handsome, strong and bold young man who could fend for himself and was afraid of nothing — not even of the

bands of robbers or the beasts of prey from which he protected his father's herds. His name was Paris.

One day, as he was grazing his cattle, three beautiful goddesses appeared before him. They were Hera, wife of Zeus, the ruler of gods and men, Pallas Athene, the goddess of wisdom and just war, and Aphrodite, the goddess of love and beauty. Paris was to decide which of them was the most beautiful, the most graceful, the most charming! Hermes himself, messenger of the gods, was sent by Zeus, mightiest of those who sit on Olympus, to set the herdsman his task. He was to give the one he judged most beautiful a golden apple from the garden of the Hesperides.

So Paris stood before the three naked goddesses, holding the apple in his hand and listening as one after another they promised him rich rewards. Hera offered him power and riches if he chose her, Pallas Athene offered him glory in war and Aphrodite promised him Helen, wife of Menelaus, King of Sparta, the most beautiful of all mortal women. Without hesitation, Paris gave Aphrodite the golden apple, and from that moment on she protected him from all harm, while he earned the bitter hatred of Hera and Pallas Athene.

It was not long before King Priam held a series of magnificent games for his wife Hecabe. One of the prizes was to be a bullock from Paris' herd. The young herdsman took the animal to the city himself, and since he was a bold fellow and sorry to lose the bullock, he joined in the races. How surprised he was to win three times in a row. He beat everyone, even his royal brother Hector.

It was soon discovered who this unknown, handsome herdsman really was. What good fortune that the royal child who had been so mourned should have been saved! King Priam wept with joy, and his mother Hecabe would not let him out of her arms. His brothers and sisters welcomed him warmly. Only his sister Cassandra, who had the gift of prophesy, appeared sad, recalling what was to be the prince's fateful mission. But it was in vain that she warned her parents not to allow Paris into their home. They took him to the palace, and from then on he lived with the rest of them in the luxury and comfort of the royal court.

The goddess Aphrodite had not forgotten her promise. One day she appeared to Paris and told him he should set out for Sparta to the court of King Menelaus. The time was coming when he might gain Queen Helen, daughter of the ruler of the gods, Zeus himself, who had given her an almost superhuman beauty.

Until now Helen had lived in harmony and love with her husband, and had no notion of how fateful the visit of this handsome youth from the rich city of Troy was to be. They met at the banquet held by Menelaus in honour of his guest, and Paris fell in love with Helen as soon as he set eyes on her. Helen, too, fell victim to his charms; he enchanted her, turned her head and kindled the flames of passion in her. So at the first opportunity, when Menelaus was obliged to sail for Crete, the two of them boarded a ship and eloped. Aphrodite sent them a following wind, and after a safe voyage of only three days, Helen entered the gates of Troy at Paris' side.

The news of their flight caused an uproar

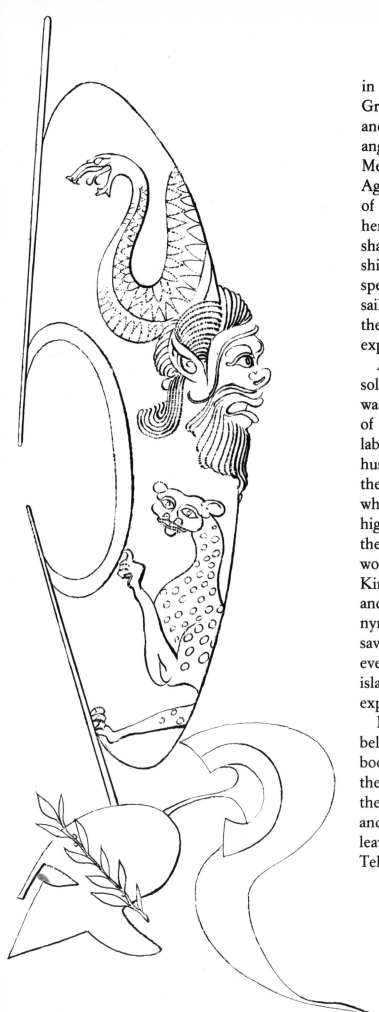

in Sparta and throughout the whole of Greece. The rulers of all the Greek states and kingdoms were filled with outrage and angrily pledged their support for King Menelaus, who together with his brother Agamemnon began to prepare a campaign of vengeance against Troy. The Greek heroes and rulers made ready for war. They sharpened their swords, strengthened their shields and helmets, and sharpened their spears and lances. Ships were fitted out and sails woven. The warriors made their way to the port of Aulis, from where the Greek expedition was to set sail for Troy.

Among their ranks were countless fine soldiers and heroes of great renown. There was Idomeneus, ruler of Crete and grandson of King Minos, builder of the famous labyrinth, Agamemnon of Mycenae and husband of Helen's sister Clytemnestra; with them sailed the old King of Pylos, Nestor, whose wisdom and prudence were held in high esteem throughout the land. Then there was the hero Philoctetes, heir to the wondrous arrows of Heracles, Ajax, the King of Salamis' son, famed for his strength, and Achilles, son of King Peleus and the sea nymph Thetis, whose body was invulnerable save for a single spot on his heel. And eventually even the young king of the rocky island of Ithaca, Odysseus, joined the expedition, too.

Many of these heroes were filled with belligerent zeal, greedy for honours and rich booty; only Odysseus, most resourceful of all the rulers and heroes, was reluctant to join the campaign. He had only recently married, and had a small son at home. Was he to leave his beloved Penelope and little Telemachus to go to war? He could not bear

the thought, so he used his cunning wits. When the messengers arrived from Menelaus to ask his help, they found the King of Ithaca in the fields. He was walking behind a plough to which a horse and an ox were harnessed, and instead of grain he was sowing salt. He appeared confused as he answered all their questions and appeals. The messengers thought that he had lost his senses. And the plan almost came off.

But one of the messengers was suspicious. He knew that Odysseus was clever, and felt that he might be trying to trick them. He seized the king's son Telemachus and laid the child in the furrow right in the path of the horse and ox. At that instant Odysseus stopped his ploughing and ran to his son. Out of his mind, indeed! No, he was simply pretending to be mad, and now he had given himself away there was nothing for it but to join the Greeks in their great expedition.

But the start of the campaign against Troy was far from being an auspicious one.

When, in answer to the call from the wronged Menelaus and wise Nestor, almost twelve hundred ships and around a hundred thousand warriors gathered at the port of Aulis, a commander-in-chief had to be appointed. The one chosen for this post was Agamemnon, King of Mycenae, a brave man, but nonetheless short-tempered and intolerant. Before they set sail, he decided a burnt offering should be made to the gods, that they might look upon the enterprise with favour. To everyone's dismay a huge red snake appeared beneath a big plane tree at the place of sacrifice. It leapt into the tree and killed eight young birds in their nest, along with their mother, before turning to stone itself.

The soothsayer Calchas, who was also taking part in the expedition, explained to the Greeks what this meant. It was a sign from the gods, he said, that the Achaean army would fight for nine years, until Troy was finally conquered in the tenth.

Yet that was not to be the last of the dreadful omens.

The Achaeans raised their masts and hoisted their sails, but try as they might, they were unable to reach the open sea. In vain the helmsmen turned their rudders hither and thither trying to catch a wind. Not even the lightest breeze obliged. When Agamemnon, as commander-in-chief, turned once more to Calchas to ask what this might mean, he was told that they were becalmed because of the wrath of the goddess Artemis, for the Mycenaean king had once killed one of her sacred hinds. Her anger would only be appeased by sacrificing the king's lovely daughter Iphigenia to her. Agamemnon was griefstricken to hear these words, and was about to leave the expedition. But Iphigenia herself decided to sacrifice her life, in order to meet the angry goddess' demands. She was no sooner on the altar than a thick black cloud suddenly appeared. And, quite hidden from view, Artemis carried Agamemnon's daughter away to the far-off land of Tauris, where the girl became her priestess. As the cloud moved away, a hind could be seen on the altar instead of Iphigenia. The prophet Calchas soon joyfully announced that the goddess had been appeased.

And so it turned out. In a short while a favourable wind was blowing. Their sails filled, the huge fleet quickly raised anchor and set sail immediately for Asia Minor.

As the Greeks landed on the shores beneath the huge ramparts of the city, the Trojans were waiting with their weapons at the ready. They knew well enough the prophesy that the first Achaean to touch Trojan soil would pay for it with his life.

Odysseus, too, knew the prophesy, but he was anxious to prove his valour. So he first threw his shield ashore, and then jumped onto it. The next to jump ashore onto the bare ground was Prince Protesilaus, and the prophesy was fulfilled, for he fell, struck by Hector's spear. His death was like a signal for the first bloody battle to begin. The ranks of the two armies met in a ferocious clash, and Greek and Trojan blood stained the ground.

The terrible, unrelenting, merciless war had begun.

How bitterly truthful Calchas' words were to prove . . .

For ten long years young blood continued to flow on both sides — and all because of one woman. For ten long years the Greek forces besieged Troy, and for ten long years the city defended itself with all its might. Even the gods of Olympus were involved. The Greeks were helped by Hera and Pallas Athene, who were angry with Paris; they also enjoyed the favour of the mighty sea-god Poseidon and Hermes, the divine messenger, to name but a few. On the Trojans' side stood Apollo and the fierce god of war, Ares, Artemis, goddess of the hunt, and of course the goddess Aphrodite. Many other members of the great family of gods up on Olympus took sides. Cruel battles claimed the lives of Paris' heroic brother, Hector, and Achilles, the bravest of the Greeks. He was killed by an arrow which

Paris shot into the one spot where Achilles could be wounded, his heel. Paris died, too, poisoned by an arrow from the bow of Philoctetes; yet Troy held out . . .

Glory, success, heroic deeds — everything had failed. The city was undefeated; all direct attacks had proved worthless. Only one weapon remained, one of which the King of Ithaca was master: cunning.

And slowly an idea began to take shape in Odysseus' mind . . .

In front of the gates of Troy there suddenly appeared a huge wooden horse. The Trojans could have had no idea that the Greeks had built it on the instructions of Odysseus, or that the best of the Greek warriors, King Menelaus, Idomeneus, Philoctetes, Odysseus and others, were hidden inside it. They just saw the horse, standing near the walls, the Greeks leaving their camp, burning their scaffolding, boarding their ships and sailing away. The Trojans began to cheer. Clearly the Greeks had abandoned all hope of conquering Troy — they were leaving the battlefield! The Trojans began to stroll across the plains outside their city, where recently much blood has been spilled. They examined the wooden horse more closely, wondering what they should do with it. Some felt it should be hurled into the sea, while many wanted to drag it into the city, to be kept as a reminder to all that the enemy had been defeated.

Quite suddenly, out of the bushes, there stepped a wretched-looking old man. His hands bound, he was weeping most fearfully, begging for mercy. Mumbling and stammering, he told of how he had just managed to escape from the Greeks, who

had tied him up, leaving him to die of starvation. The Trojan leaders questioned him, and discovered that his name was Sinon; they promised to spare him if he told them where the wooden horse came from, and why the Achaeans had built it. Sinon paused for a moment — before revealing that it was a gift to appease Pallas Athene, who was angry with the Greeks because Odysseus had carried off her sacred statue from the temple in Troy. If the horse were to replace the Palladium, the goddess would be sure to offer the Trojans her protection. This was, of course, not true, but the Trojans believed Sinon. They all began shouting that the horse should be taken behind the walls and placed on the sacred hill, the Acropolis. Amidst the uproar the warning voice of the priest Laocoon could just be heard.

"Wait! The Greeks cannot be trusted, even when they bear gifts; this is some treachery!" These doom-ridden words had scarcely been uttered, when two giant serpents rose out of the sea and instantly killed Laocoon and his two sons.

For a moment some of the Trojans were stunned into silence. But Sinon raised his arms above his head and cried: "See how the goddess has punished Laocoon because he tried to deprive her of this sacred gift!"

Now the Trojans acted quickly. Some hurried over to the horse, while others turned to destroy part of the ramparts which for so long have held the Greeks at bay. And through this opening they dragged the wooden horse.

On they went until, with the horse, they reached the top of the hill, the Acropolis! And with whoops and cries of joy that the siege was finally over, the people ran from house to house, embracing one another. Celebration banquets were prepared with the richest foods and the finest wines.

There stood the wooden horse, inside the ramparts; the trap set by Odysseus was about to close on its victims. The last night of the glorious city of Troy was at hand.

As the Trojans lay down to sleep, the Greeks waited for the agreed signal. Then, suddenly, armed warriors rushed from the

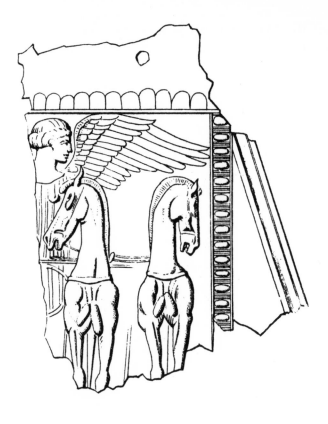

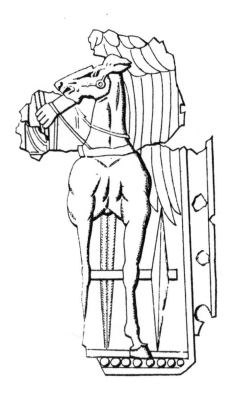

horse's stomach. They ran amok in the city, setting fire to thatched roofs, destroying houses, slaughtering men and women alike. In the meantime more warriors hurried ashore from their ships, which had been hidden from view behind an offshore island. The work of destruction was quickly

accomplished. King Priam and all his sons lay slain. Troy in flames was razed to the ground. The only one of its defenders to be saved was Aeneas, who carried his father Anchises and his son Ascanius from the blazing ruins.

The booty was unbounded. The Greek ships were filled with gold, silver, rare cloths and slaves. And slowly, the last flames died down over the city.

The Trojan war was at an end, but the trials and tribulations of those who took part in it were to continue.

The gods did not allow all the warriors to return home safely. Menelaus of Sparta carried away his Helen, but because he forgot to offer a sacrifice to show his gratitude to the gods, he was fated to roam the seas for eight years before landing again on the shores of his homeland. And an even worse destiny awaited Agamemnon. His cousin Aegisthus had taken advantage of the king's long absence from the rich state of Mycenae, usurped the throne and taken Agamemnon's wife Clytemnestra. When the hero returned from Troy he was treacherously slain at a banquet.

And what of the man whose ingenuity had given the Greeks their long-awaited victory?

When Odysseus and his twelve ships sailed away from the smouldering ruins of Troy, he could have had no idea that it would be a long time before he was to step ashore on his native Ithaca, that many dangers still awaited him, endless wanderings, and frequent struggles for his life. Seven years after the fall of Troy, Odysseus sits on the seashore, gazing into the distance and longing to be home in Ithaca; his eyes are glistening with tears.

He is a prisoner of the beautiful daughter of the Titan Atlas, the nymph Calypso, who has fallen in love with him. But he is indifferent to the comfort in which he lives, ungrateful for the care bestowed upon him by the ruler of the island of Ogygia, deaf to her promises of eternal youth and immortality, should he agree to stay with her on the island for ever. He has no wish to be a captive of beauty. More and more often he sits alone beside the sea, longing to catch sight of the merest wisp of smoke rising above the horizon from distant Ithaca.

It is there that his one desire lies, to Penelope and his son Telemachus that his thoughts turn. He has but one wish: to set foot once again on Ithaca, just once more to embrace his wife and son; then, if need be, he would die . . .

The House Without Its Master

The Decision of Zeus

Zeus, father of gods and men, lord of Mount Olympus, mightiest of the gods, held a feast to which all the gods and goddesses were invited. All gathered around his golden throne, from the mightiest gods to the humblest nymphs and spirits. Only one member of that great family was absent, and that was Poseidon, brother of Zeus and ruler of the seas, who at that time dwelt at the other end of the Earth, with the Ethiopians.

As usual, the conversation turned to mortals and their destinies, and to how they often complained that all the evil on Earth was the fault of the gods and their harsh treatment of mankind. Zeus did not like to hear such things. Were the gods responsible for all earthly woes and suffering? On the contrary — most of these were brought upon mortals by their failure to hear the counsel of the gods, or by their own

arrogance or even their refusal to believe in the gods. Thus spoke Zeus, and the other gods agreed. Except, that is, for Zeus' best-loved child, the bright-eyed Pallas Athene.

"Father of us all, and ruler of gods and men; there is surely much truth in what you say," she said, daring to defy the mightiest of the Olympians. "But sometimes those who do not deserve it suffer, too. I know of one such, and am sorry for him. Poor Odysseus — what has *he* done to deserve such a fate? Has he not always honoured you, has he not always offered the most suitable of sacrifices? Yet now he is obliged to live on the island of Ogygia, and may not return home! Why are you so angry with him, lord of Olympus?"

The words of his beloved daughter vexed Zeus.

"What is this you are saying, my child: why should I be angry with Odysseus? *I* have nothing against him. It is my brother Poseidon, ruler of all the seas, who shakes the land in his anger, and prevents him from going home. Do not forget how Odysseus hurt his son Polyphemus, mightiest of the Cyclops! This is the source of Poseidon's unrelenting wrath."

"And is Odysseus to atone for his deed for

ever? That would be too cruel a fate. You, lord of lords, should consider what can be done for him, if only for the sake of Penelope and Telemachus. What is happening in Odysseus' palace is just too much to bear."

"I know — they all believe that Odysseus is dead, and one suitor after another is paying his respects to Penelope."

"Not only that, but they behave as though the palace belonged to them! They hold feasts every day, slaughter the best cattle; they behave in a high-handed way and order everyone around. Penelope is too weak to oppose them, and Telemachus too young to take them on. There are more than a hundred of them already! Father, allow Odysseus to return to put things right!"

"You are right," Zeus replied. "And it is a good thing that Poseidon is not here at our banquet. If those of us who are here agree to help Odysseus, he will be helpless against us. Hermes, ambassador of my will, prepare to make a journey! Go to Ogygia and tell the nymph Calypso to set Odysseus free at once."

"Thank you for your wise decision," said Pallas Athene. "But, mightiest of the mighty, we must help not only Odysseus, but also his son. Permit me to visit Ithaca in disguise and advise that inexperienced young fellow a little."

"As you wish," Zeus replied, and a ray of hope shone on Odysseus' fate.

Pallas Athene's Advice

With a single leap the goddess Pallas Athene descended from Olympus to Ithaca, arriving in the royal palace. She disguised herself as a chieftain and was warmly greeted by Telemachus.

The scene in Odysseus' palace was reminiscent of a beehive. Penelope's suitors, in high spirits, were enjoying themselves in the courtyard, playing dice, drinking wine, singing, dancing, and ordering all sorts of delicacies — the servants were nearly run off their feet. By now many of the suitors could scarcely speak coherently, but they were making a terrible hubbub just the same.

"What is going on here?" asked Pallas Athene, disguised as the chieftain. "Where have all these people come from? Why are they acting like this? It is no way for friends

tell you what I heard when I sailed with my ship to fetch cargo. Your father is alive and well, but a prisoner on one of the islands in the middle of the sea. I have known your father for many years; I am amazed to see how like him you are, and I am sure he will manage to escape somehow. For he is no fool, and the gods will not show him disfavour for ever. He will certainly return, and I think it

to behave — they are turning the house upside down! If your father Odysseus were here, he would make short shrift of them!"

"If my father were here, all would be different!" sighed Telemachus. "But so many years have gone by since the fall of Troy, and I do not know what has happened to him, whether he is indeed dead, or what fate has overtaken him. All these who meet here in our palace day after day have long since forgotten about him. They pay court to my mother, and each of them would like to marry her; but they all eat our food, slaughter our cattle, drink the wine from our vines, as if it all belonged to them."

"My dear Telemachus, you mustn't let them get away with it," interrupted Pallas Athene, in the voice of the chieftain. "I will

will be soon; but you must not rely only on his coming home. You must set things to rights yourself, and as soon as possible! Take to heart the advice I give you. Summon all the suitors who have invited themselves to your house, and tell them to go back to where they came from. Then take a good ship, sail quickly to Pylos to old King Nestor, and then to Menelaus of Sparta — for they fought alongside your father. They are sure to know something of him and can advise you how to deal with these arrogant and ill-mannered suitors. For you are a boy no more, and you can no longer merely weep and lament over what is going on here! Act like a man!"

Telemachus listened carefully to these words of the chieftain, and decided to do as he was advised. The very next day he called his mother's troublesome suitors together and forbade them once and for all to set foot in the palace. Let them feast where they would! Let them be each other's guests! Let them slay their own bullocks, let them drink their own wine!

Telemachus would put up with their dissoluteness no more!

And Pallas Athene vanished like a bird.

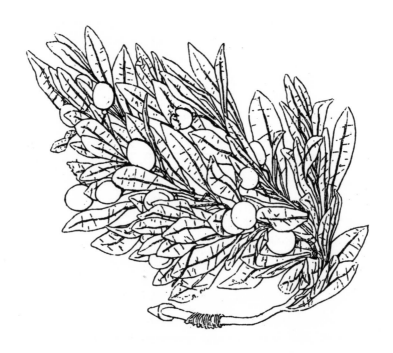

A Council on Ithaca

When the goddess Eos lit up the morning star in the east, Odysseus' son rose from his bed, donned his ceremonial robes, buckled on his sword, and ordered the heralds to summon all the noblemen. The goddess Pallas Athene bathed him in shining light, and when he sat upon his father's throne, everyone stared at him in wonder. A council was to be held on Ithaca after such a long time? How had Odysseus' son reached such a decision?

"Perhaps he wants to give us news of Odysseus — what if he has heard that he is returning after all, perhaps with an army, and wants to make a solemn announcement?" some of them thought, and old Aegyptos even spoke their thoughts out loud. But they heard different words.

"I do not wish to speak of my father, men of Ithaca, or of his return," Telemachus told the gathering. "But rather of what is taking place in his home *now*. Odysseus was a good ruler, and a kind father to you all. Why then have you wormed your way into his house? Who gave you the right to destroy his property? Are you not afraid that your shameful deeds might bring down upon you the wrath of the gods? Are you quite insensitive to both my mother and to me? Begone with you!"

Telemachus' bold accusations took everyone's breath away for an instant. They were not used to such words, and so suddenly they were speechless. Only one, the most troublesome of all the suitors, one Antinous, an arrogant, haughty and inconsiderate fellow, grew angry at what he heard.

"So you would send us away from the palace, Telemachus? Do you not know that you have insulted us all?" he cried.

"You complain that your mother's suitors are parasites in this palace. But kindly bear in mind that it is her fault entirely. She has had us on a piece of string for nearly four years now, promising first one and then the other, and never deciding between us. She wanted us to wait, not to insist that she remarry, although Odysseus was long dead, for sure. She said she would choose one of us, but we were to be patient, and wait until she had woven cloth for the shroud of Odysseus' father, old Laertes. How resourceful Penelope is! We all know well enough how that turned out! She thought she would get the better of us if she unravelled at night what she had woven during the day! For three years she fooled us, until one of her servants gave her away. Then we caught her at it! But I tell you,

Telemachus, we will not move from this house until it is clear whom she has chosen for her husband!"

As the dispute continued, amidst the bustle and the din which were suddenly unleashed, one of the Ithacan noblemen, old Halitherses, noticed a group of eagles flying over the council chamber. They looked menacing, flapping their wings wildly and fighting among themselves, until it was a wonder they did not peck each other to death. Halitherses knew how to interpret the birds' strange flight; had he not foretold to Odysseus much of what happened at Troy? When he saw the eagles over the royal castle, his face clouded deeply.

"Friends, this does not augur well. You will remember what I prophesied to Odysseus when he left for Troy with Agamemnon's army? That much suffering would come his way, that his friends and those close to him would die, but that after twenty years he would return home. I warn you — that moment is now at hand; Odysseus is not far away, and will return, and you will not even recognise him! And he will wreak vengeance on all those who

have brought dishonour on his son, his wife and those who are faithful to him!"

"Go and tell your tales to the children," sneered another of Penelope's unruly suitors. "A few birds fly past the window, and you have to see a sign from the gods! What nonsense! Odysseus is dead and buried long ago — and you should be, too! At least Telemachus could be spared your nonsensical predictions. He's angry enough as it is! But let Penelope go to her father and ask him for a dowry, and let her marry someone at last, or there will be no peace here!"

Telemachus saw that there was no way he was going to deal amicably with so many arrogant wooers. But the chieftain's visit had convinced him that his father was still alive. He was certain he would find some clue as to his whereabouts.

"Enough, enough," he replied, calmly, but firmly. "It seems you are not satisfied with having wasted nearly all our wealth; you would have the kingdom to boot! And you suppose me still to be a small and helpless child. I am alone against you all; but do not think you will have it all your own way. I will go out into the world to find out what has happened to my father. If he is not alive, I will return and make a funeral sacrifice for him, and my mother will remarry. But if I should find that he is alive, then I will call

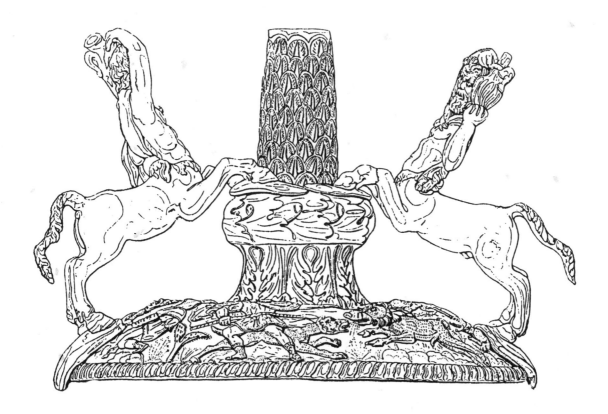

upon Zeus every day that I may repay you with interest for all you have done to me."

These bold words again silenced many of the suitors, but the insolent and ruthless Antinous scowled at young Telemachus once again.

"What makes you suddenly so brave, young fellow? Do you really suppose you can frighten us? Take care, lest you end up like your father! You, too, could get lost in the world! But go your way as you please; we won't worry over it. Can you smell something? There's a boar roasting for us outside! And the servant-girls are already pouring the wine!"

Telemachus was stung bitterly by these words, but he saw that he was not yet in any position to oppose his enemies by force. So he left them alone and went to see his old nurse Eurycleia, keeper of the palace keys. He wanted her to help him prepare stores for his journey, and to do so in the utmost secrecy. He and his friends would go out to find his father; and find him they would, even if it meant a journey to the ends of the Earth!

When Eurycleia heard what her beloved Telemachus had in mind, she burst into tears. She tried hard to dissuade him, warned him of the dangers of such an enterprise, and of the intrigues his enemies were sure to enter into against him.

But Telemachus would not listen; he begged of his faithful servant, his old nurse, only one thing: not to say a word about his plans to his mother Penelope. He wished to spare her the pain of taking leave of him. Eurycleia was to tell her only after eleven days, provided his mother did not miss him sooner. The faithful nurse had to swear to obey Telemachus.

The very same evening, when the sun had set and shadows engulfed the city, Telemachus' friends gathered at the harbour, where a ship was ready and waiting. Pallas Athene herself had called them together and taken them to the ship; on all Penelope's suitors she laid a deep sleep, so that Telemachus' company might leave safely.

Then, disguised as a trusted friend of Odysseus and adviser to the young Telemachus, Pallas Athene, or 'Mentor', stepped on board and sat in the stern beside Telemachus.

When they had had cast off, raised the mast and hoisted the sail, a sharp westerly breeze got up. It was the god Zephyrus answering the call of Pallas Athene, and he drove Telemachus' boat all the way to its destination.

Nestor

Telemachus arrived in Pylos, seat of old King Nestor, just as celebrations were being held in honour of Zeus, king of the gods.

Telemachus was not too sure of himself, for it was the first time he had been engaged in such dealings on his own. And this king was so renowned, for despite his great age, he had excelled at the siege of Troy. Is there any wonder Telemachus was shy? That he was afraid he would not find the right words to say to the venerable old man, already ruling a third generation of his subjects?

Pallas Athene herself again had to encourage him and give him confidence.

"You look very sheepish, Telemachus; but now your shyness must be put aside," the goddess, still accompanying him disguised as Mentor, told him. "I know young people are often shy when they must ask their elders for advice or help. But you know what it is you want! You have come to seek news of your father, and Nestor was for many years his comrade in arms. He will surely understand, and will tell you everything he knows of his fate!"

"It is easy enough for you to say that," sighed Telemachus, "but how am I to know how to speak correctly to a man of such renown? And how will he receive us?"

"Do not worry! You spoke to your mother's suitors like a man when you had to! You will think of something — the gods will help you out! Now you can sit back and let them do the work!"

And they did.

Nestor received Telemachus and his companions most warmly. He told his son Peisistratus to lead his guests to places of honour beside him, so that he might choose for them the tastiest pieces of meat, and fill their cups with the best wine. He asked Mentor, as the older of his guests, to give a toast in honour of Poseidon, the sea god. Then he asked Telemachus to do the same. Both of them did as the king asked them, and according to the ancient custom they begged Poseidon to show favour to Nestor and his family.

And, quite suddenly, Telemachus' shyness left him altogether. He had no difficulty at all in finding words; they came to his lips of their own accord, and they sounded eloquent and full of dignity — so much so that all were surprised at the pleasant and charming manner of this young man.

Then old Nestor said:

"Now that we have heard the toasts, which I am sure were to the liking of the lord of the seas and waters, the moment has come for me to ask who you are and where you come from, my friends. Have you come here by chance, or is there some purpose to your visit?"

At that moment Telemachus felt the encouraging touch of Mentor's hand on his arm, and he stood up and said:

"Renowned King Nestor, most honoured of all the Greek rulers, you have welcomed us with kindness and warmth, for which we thank you sincerely! You ask what brings us here. Well, you should know that we have sailed from Ithaca in a black ship with a red-painted prow; we do not come to discuss matters of state, but on private business, to see if we may find out something of the fate of my father, Odysseus. You fought together — along with many other Greeks — at Troy, but the war has long since ended and we still have no news of my father. You must surely know what has become of him if anyone does. Is he alive? Or is he dead? Or is he so troubled that he is unable to return? These are the questions that I would put to you, my lord, and I beg of you, if you know anything of my father, tell me the truth!"

"Then you are the son of my old comrade Odysseus?" whispered Nestor, with deep feeling; and he shook his head as he immersed himself in memories of times past. "Ah, the things your father and I have lived through at Troy! You might sit for five years, my boy, and I should still have tales to tell of our trials in that fearful war, and of your father, with whom none on that expedition could compare in cunning. So many died in battle — the glorious Achilles,

Ajax, my brave son Antilochus, Patroclus and Agamemnon. But as for your father, I truly do not know. I can say one thing only, that no one was more favoured by the gods than he. I have, however, heard what is happening in his house. It is terrible, but since I know him to be a favourite of the gods, I am sure he will return and mete out to that band of your mother's suitors the punishment they deserve."

"If only you might be right, my lord," sighed Telemachus, "and if only I might know where to seek my father, so that I might tell him all this!"

"In this, Telemachus, I cannot be of any assistance," the old King of Pylos told him. "But may I offer you this advice. Go to Menelaus in Sparta; he returned from Troy only recently, for he has been wandering over land and sea for the past seven years. He is most likely to know something of Odysseus. Who knows — perhaps he even met him on his journeys. Anyway, he is sure to tell you the truth if you explain your situation. But do not stay away from home too long, for you are needed on Ithaca! Those wretched suitors will surely try to divide the whole kingdom amongst themselves while you are away!"

Telemachus thanked King Nestor. Anxious to find at last some clue to his father's whereabouts, he prepared to leave immediately. But the old king would not hear of it.

"Surely you do not want people to say that Nestor could not even offer shelter to the son of the famed Odysseus? I should be ashamed; no, this cannot be. You will spend the night in my palace and have a good rest. In the morning I will have a fast team of

horses prepared for you, and my son Peisistratus will accompany you to Menelaus."

"These are the words of a great ruler," added Pallas Athene, who still accompanied Telemachus disguised as Mentor, the old family friend. "Let Telemachus get his strength back in your house, my lord, and I will return to the ship to encourage our

companions. They are still boys, all nearly as young as Telamachus himself, and they set out with us only out of love for him and for his father."

All were amazed at the words of Telemachus' companion, and they were even more amazed when, as he was leaving, he turned into an eagle and vanished from their sight.

"The gods are on your side after all," old Nestor proclaimed. "Be grateful, and show yourself worthy of their favour. That was

surely Pallas Athene herself, daughter of Zeus, who has taken you under her protection. If only she would show such favour to me and my children! Tomorrow I will have a fat cow sacrificed to her; she likes that best of all."

And in the rosy glow of dawn the next morning, Nestor held a great sacrificial ceremony. The fattest of all the cows, its horns decorated according to the ancient custom, was prepared for the sacrifice. It was washed with water and barley seed, and a tuft of its coat was thrown into the fire. Then the king's son Thrasymedes stunned the beast with an axe, while the youngest of his sons, Peisistratus, drew a knife.

Dark red blood flowed, and the heifer fell to the ground. They took the best meat from the rump and rubbed it with lard, and began to roast it on the open fire, basting it with rare wine. The wine was eleven years old and the tastiest the king's cellars could offer. The meat was turned on long forks over the flames, and warm thanks were offered to the goddess Athene.

Everyone feasted thus for a long time, until they had eaten every last morsel. Then Nestor's daughter prepared a bath for

Telemachus and ordered the slaves to bath him, rub his body with fragrant oil, and dress him in a splendid new cloak. When they again lifted their cups brimming with the most delicious wine, the refreshed and rested Telemachus looked like one of the gods.

Then Odysseus' son stepped into a beautifully decorated chariot, and Nestor's son Peisistratus stepped up beside him, grasped the reins, and made ready.

The impatient team set off at a gallop, and before long the steep slopes of Pylos were lost from sight.

Menelaus of Sparta

Telemachus and Peisistratus reached the land of Sparta, full of steep hills and precipices, after two days of travel.

They made straight for the royal palace, and could hear from afar the sound of singing, music and peals of laughter. When the team halted and they leapt down from the chariot, they saw a man leading two jugglers into the palace. He stopped, looked the new arrivals up an down, and in a few moments was bowing before King Menelaus.

"There are two strangers here, my lord," he announced. "Am I to have their horses unharnessed, or am I to send them away?"

"What is this you say?" Menelaus scolded angrily. "As if you, the steward of my palace, did not know that *all* are welcome here today. For am I not celebrating the weddings of both my daughter Hermione and my bold son Megapenthes? Bring them here among the other guests! For on our journey back from Troy we ourselves were often grateful guests at the table of others! It would be shameful to send two visitors away from our door, especially since night will soon be falling!"

At these words the steward turned on his heels, ran outside and ordered the servants to attend to all the strangers' needs.

They were led to splendid rooms; servants prepared for them refreshing baths, then rubbed them with fragrant oil, dressed them in resplendent robes, and led them into the banqueting hall.

Telemachus was left breathless by the splendour of Menelaus' palace. He stared in wonder at the golden ornaments of the hall, the seats inlaid with ivory, the gilded and silvered bowls and plates set out on the tables.

Peisistratus knew the king, so he was welcomed as an old friend; the king offered

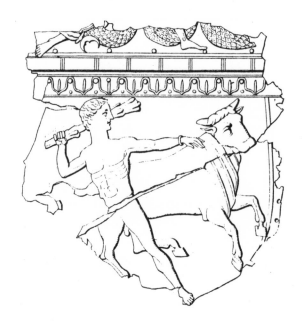

him and Telemachus the places of honour at his side. Out of courtesy he did not yet ask Telemachus his name, but only invited the two of them to eat and drink whatever they wished.

At one point Menelaus heard Telemachus whisper to Peisistratus:

"How magnificent all this is! It is like a palace on Olympus itself. Perhaps only the great Zeus has such a splendid palace, such riches!"

"My dear friend," said Menelaus, "who could compare with Zeus? I am rich, it is true, and there are few mortals who can match my wealth. But my possessions bring me little joy. What you see here has been brought from many far-off lands — from Phoenicia, from the home of the Ethiopians, from distant Libya, and from those rich places where the harvest is brought in several times a year. For eight years I wandered before I and my fleet returned home, and many of my friends and companions did not return at all. And I should rather give up a third of my booty and have beside me those who perished. I am sorry for all of them, but most of all for the one closest to my heart, the glorious and clever Odysseus. And how much greater must be the grief of Penelope, his old father Laertes, and his son Telemachus!"

Telemachus felt tears well into his eyes at these words. He hid his face behind his purple robe, and was scarcely able to contain a sob. But Menelaus did not fail to notice: he had been watching his guest attentively for some time. Whom did he remind him of? The hair, the look in those eyes — how like him he was! He was the very image of Odysseus!

He was deep in thought when, on the other side of him, Queen Helen, truly as beautiful as a goddess, leaned towards him.

"My lord, when I look at this young man who came with Peisistratus, he reminds me more and more of Odysseus. Did you not see how he almost wept when you spoke of his troubles? Something tells me that this is Odysseus' son . . ."

King Menelaus nodded his agreement, and turned to Peisistratus at once:

"Peisistratus, son of my old friend — who is this you have brought here on this joyous wedding day? This young man looks just like Odysseus. Am I mistaken, or is Telemachus indeed sitting at table with us?"

"Your eyes do not deceive you, mighty ruler," Peisistratus replied. "This is indeed Telemachus, and my father, Nestor, sends him to you, asking that you help him . . . Perhaps you can advise him. He is quite alone in the world, fatherless, with no one to help him even in his own house."

Again, tears almost welled into Menelaus' eyes.

"Welcome, Telemachus, welcome, son of my beloved comrade in arms," he said, with great feeling. "I always imagined how

I should one day reward him for all he suffered on my account, on that unfortunate Trojan campaign. I would gladly have given him half my kingdom, for without his cunning we should never have conquered Troy! But the gods decided otherwise, and it is of no use lamenting over that which we cannot change. My dear Telemachus, you have no idea how much I sympathise with you. Nor do you know how I should like to help you."

"There is only one thing I ask of you, King of Sparta — only one reason I come to you," said Telemachus. "Tell me what you know of my father! Is he no longer living? Did you see him die with your own eyes? Or do you know that he is still alive and roaming the world — perhaps far away from us? Tell me all you know, I beg of you; I do not ask for sympathy, only to know the simple truth!"

These were the words of a man; Telemachus no longer spoke as a nervous and immature boy. Menelaus was greatly impressed by his honesty.

"I know, dear son of Odysseus, that your heart is heavy. I understand your pain, particularly since I have heard of the plots against your mother, laid by some villains. I have heard how they are stealing everything they can lay their hands on. But believe me, I am convinced that your father will return one day and will seek a well-deserved revenge for all those rogues. And you must be ready for that time."

"Then have you spoken to my father recently?"

"I have not — would I not have told you so at once, seeing how you mourn over his absence? During the many years that I, too,

went wandering, I heard of Odysseus only once, and that was from the sea god Proteus," Menelaus began. "I was far away, on the shores of the land of Egypt. Through the will of the gods we had to stay there for over twenty days, tormented by hunger and thirst. Who knows how it would all have ended, had not Proteus' daughter Eidothea taken pity on me. What an unpleasant old man Proteus is! He can foretell the fates of men, but it is terribly hard to make him reveal them. If one strikes him, he changes into a snake, then into a panther, a boar — into any living creature, or even into fire, a tree — just to avoid having to tell you what

you need to know! Fortunately his daughter let us into his secret. Only at noon, when he goes down to the sea-shore to sleep, can you catch him on land and force him to reveal what the fates hold in store for you and what the intentions of the gods are. While he was in the form of a seal, I and my three most faithful companions grabbed him, and held him firm. How the old man resisted! In the end he promised to answer three questions.

"First of all I asked him why we were unable to return home, why we had been kept there as prisoners for so long. He told me it was a punishment for forgetting to offer a sacrifice to the gods as we hurried away from the ruins of Troy. If I wanted to escape, I should first return to the shores of Egypt and there offer a sacrifice to the gods.

"Then I asked about my other comrades, especially my brother Agamemnon. What I heard was terrible. I wept for a long time when I was told that he would reach Mycenae alive and well, but that his cousin Aegisthus, to whom he had delegated power in his absence, was plotting to slay him at a banquet — like a bull at the trough.

"The third time I asked about Odysseus; I can remember exactly what he said to me, and I will tell you, Telemachus, his very words. 'The son of Laertes,' he told me, 'King of Ithaca, is alive. The beautiful nymph Calypso is holding him on her island, and he has neither ship, nor companions, so he is unable to escape. He yearns for Ithaca, for his wife and son. And he is destined to see them again.'

"This is what Proteus told me, and his prophesy is certain to be true. Perhaps it will reassure you a little, Telemachus. You should stay with us a while here in Sparta, and rest. Out of long-standing friendship for your father I should like to give you some gift to take home with you. Do you know what? I will give you three thoroughbred horses, a burnished chariot, and a gilded cup! Stay awhile!"

But the news he had just heard of his father made Telemachus all the more restless and impatient. He was anxious to return to his mother. He could not stop thinking about her, and about her shameless suitors, who were capable of anything.

"Thank you, my lord; I should like to stay here with you, perhaps for a whole year, and to listen to the story of what you have lived through during the war and after it. But what if my father is at this moment on his way home; what if my mother needs my help? What if those irksome suitors of hers

are plotting some new treachery? Thank you, too, for your kind offer of gifts — but I have already received from you the greatest gift you could have offered me. It would be quite enough for you to give me the gilded cup you spoke of. It will always remind me of the kind welcome I received here."

"But you must stay for a few days at least, Telemachus; you would surely not offend me! I have a proposal: you shall spend twelve days here, resting and regaining your strength for the struggle which awaits you at home. Then you shall go where your duty to your family takes you. I think your father would not do otherwise in your place."

These words of King Menelaus moved Telemachus.

He realised he could not refuse entirely the invitation of such an old friend of his father's.

"Twelve days, then," he said, bowing his head, and a smile of satisfaction spread over Menelaus' face.

And in the evening, as he lay down beside Queen Helen, the Spartan king murmured, his voice cracked with emotion:

"He is a true son of his father. Royal blood truly flows through his veins."

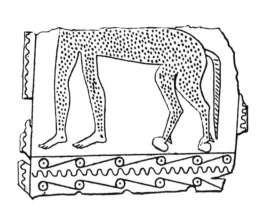

Intrigues

While Telemachus was travelling across Pylos and Sparta, back in Odysseus' house Penelope's importunate suitors, led by Antinous and Eurymachus, were on the rampage. They carried on as if nothing had happened, feasting, holding games, getting drunk. But what an uproar there was, what outrage when they learned that young Telemachus had indeed set out to find his father! They had supposed he was buried deep in the country somewhere, among the herdsmen, that he had crawled off to them like a beaten dog — and now this! As ever, the angriest of them all was Antinous.

"So our little boy has vanished," he raged. "He is bent on drowning himself, for sure!

And he has even taken his friends along with him! He'll be sorry — we'll lie in wait for him when he returns, and get rid of him once and for all. Do you know the rocky isle of Asteris, between Same and Ithaca? It's just the place to settle our accounts with him. I'll have a ship made ready, and a score of the most valiant will came along with me!

But not a word of this in front of Penelope. She mustn't know that her son's doom is sealed."

They made all their preparations in secrecy, and were sure that Penelope suspected nothing. But one of them, whose name was Medon, took pity on her. He went to her in secret and told her what fearful deed her suitors, led by Antinous, were about to commit. It was as though Penelope had suddenly been stabbed through the heart with a dagger. She collapsed in tears, and for a long time would not be comforted.

How could her beloved son set out on such a perilous journey? She wept on and on; it was terrible to behold. If only she had known in time! If he had talked to her! She had already lost her husband, and now cruel fate was about to tear away her son!

Her servants tried in vain to comfort her. She wailed more and more, until Eurycleia, whose heart was moved by her tears, could remain silent no longer.

"I knew all about it," she confessed, tearfully. "Plunge a dagger into my heart this minute, or cast me out; punish me as you will — only forgive me for not telling you. But it was only because I had to swear to Telemachus. He did not want you to grieve over his parting — and anyway, my lady, you would not have weakened his resolve. And do not weep, Penelope. Take heart, and call upon Pallas Athene, daughter of Zeus, who will surely not allow anything to happen to your son. She will save him!"

Penelope did not reply, only ordering her servants to take her to her bed. They tried to persuade her to eat, but she refused; they brought her a jug of fresh water, but she would not drink a drop. Once more she trembled with fear, lest her beloved son should fall into the trap set by her enraged wooers. In the end she fell asleep.

The sobs and tears of this poor woman reached up to the heights of Olympus, and Pallas Athene resolved to relieve her fear and grief. She made a likeness of Penelope's sister, and sent it to her bedside.

"Do not weep, sister," the vision told her. "Grieve no more. Your grief will change nothing, and it is not called for, since the gods have nothing against Telemachus, and he is sure to return safely. You need have no fear. Pallas Athene has sent me to comfort and to calm you."

What more joyful words might Penelope have heard? If Pallas Athene was to hold a protective hand over her son, then indeed she might be at ease. She felt great relief, and stretched out her hand to the vision which quivered beside her bed.

"But if the goddess promises to protect and preserve my son, then let her tell me what has become of my husband, of my dear Odysseus. Let her give me a sign at least — has he passed into the underworld, to the realm of shadows of the god Hades? Or is he alive, somewhere far away, with the sun shining upon him? Tell me, sister, tell me . . ."

But the vision was silent; suddenly, it began to melt away, until it vanished altogether.

But at the very moment Penelope awoke from her half-sleep, half-dream, refreshed and strengthened in will, the ship carrying Antinous and the wrathful suitors was passing the island of Asteris, in the straits between Same and Ithaca.

There they lay in wait for Telemachus, impatient to accomplish their mission.

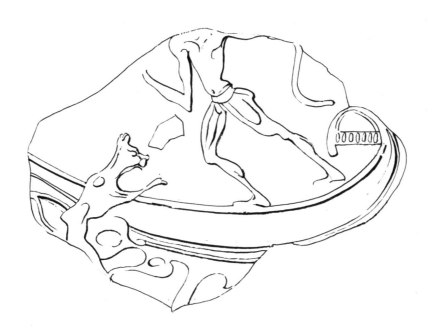

The Adventures
of Odysseus

Odysseus is Freed

Zeus had ordered his messenger, Hermes, to visit the nymph Calypso. Hermes put on his golden, winged sandals, so that he was able to fly through the air like a bird, took the magic wand with which he was able to put people to sleep or wake them up, flew like the wind across land and sea, and landed on the island of Ogygia.

It was a truly splendid sight. In the branches of the groves of ash and aspen sea birds flew hither and thither; the hillsides were covered in rich vines heavy with full, ripe grapes, and there were lush meadows filled with flowers. Four small streams moistened the earth with crystal-clear water.

From the cave where Calypso lived the scent of cedar logs and juniper carried into the distance. A tall fire burned there, and beside it sat the beautiful nymph, with her long and lovely plaits of hair, singing to herself.

The heart of Hermes leaped with joy at the sight of that delightful corner of the Earth. But the task with which his master had entrusted him gave him a good deal less satisfaction, and he was reluctant to fulfil it. What was he to do — could anyone disobey the orders of Zeus, even if he was one of the gods himself, even if he was a son of Zeus, as Hermes was? With a heavy heart he told

the nymph the will of the lord of Olympus.

"Goddess Calypso, O beautiful nymph, I bear you a message from Zeus himself. One of those who fought at the city of Troy dwells here. It is full seven years since a storm drove Odysseus here upon the shores of Ogygia. Now it is the will of Zeus that you set him free: do not keep him here; the gods want him to return home."

What terrible news this was for Calypso! It was the worst thing that might have happened. Odysseus, her beloved Odysseus, to whom she had offered her hand in marriage, so that he might gain the immortality and eternal youth she herself enjoyed, was to leave.

"How like you gods of Olympus!" she cried out in her grief. "Only you are capable of such cruelty. Do you so envy me for finding a man among the mortals? One whom I wish to take as my husband? Who was it who saved his life? I dragged him from the sea, whose waves had carried him half-dead to my island; it was *I* who nursed him! And now you would take him from me! Why should I let him go?"

"Because it is the will of Zeus — and you well know that you cannot go against it,"

said Hermes. "Otherwise you will incur his fearful wrath . . . But you can do what you will — I have delivered the message."

He vanished, leaving the unhappy Calypso alone.

For a long time she grieved, but she knew she must obey the will of Zeus, so she gathered her strength and walked from her cave down to the shore.

"Odysseus, my loved one: grieve no more. I know where your heart lies, and I will hold you here no more. Make yourself a raft of wood, and I will give you food and drink for the journey, and a new cloak, and send you home to your native Ithaca. You long for it so, and the will of the gods is mightier than I."

For a moment Odysseus was taken aback.

"What are you suggesting, Calypso? That I am to set sail on a mere raft?" he gasped. "Alone, on a few tree trunks, when not even ships dare sail the wild waters here? Is this some scheme to be rid of me?"

"My dear Odysseus, what can you be thinking of? Heaven and Earth shall be my witness that I am merely fulfilling the will of the gods. Surely you do not think I would add to your sufferings? Even so, you will have to suffer many trials and tribulations before you reach the land of your father! Only I do not know why you prefer Penelope to me. Am I less beautiful than she?"

"Forgive me, noble nymph. You are a goddess, and will remain for ever young, and surely Penelope cannot match you in beauty. But as you see, it is she for whom I yearn, whom I wish to see again and hold in my arms — even if it means adding more trials to all those I have already undergone!"

The nymph Calypso was saddened by these words, but what could she do? For the last time she prepared supper for Odysseus, for the last time she embraced him lovingly, and when the night brought forth a new dawn, she offered to help him build his raft.

First of all she gave him a large bronze axe, sharpened on both sides and with a sturdy handle of olive wood. Then she led him across the island to a place where aspen, ash and fir trees, most suitable for building a raft, were to be found. While Odysseus was cutting the trees down, she brought him all that he might need to construct his raft. When he had cut himself a mast and yard, and fixed beams around the sides of the raft's floor, Odysseus made a rudder and then lined the vessel with willow switches to protect it from the pounding of the waves.

Meanwhile, Calypso had brought him good strong canvas, and from it the King of Ithaca skilfully made the sails. On the fourth day the work was completed, and he launched the raft in the calm waters of the bay. Calypso gave him new clothes for the journey, and two skins filled to the brim — one with wine, the other with pure water from the stream.

It was with a heavy heart that she took her leave of Odysseus after such a long time, but, remembering the orders of Zeus, she sent a following wind after him, and advised him to sail with the constellation of Orion to his left and Bootes in front of him. If he kept going in that direction he would reach the island of Scheria, where the happy Phaeacian people lived. And who better to help him on his way than these splendid mariners, living in eternal peace, and willing

to assist all who were assailed by a treacherous storm?

And so Odysseus set sail.

For seventeen days he enjoyed fair weather: the skies were clear and the sea calm. On the eighteenth he sighted the outline of land rising above the horizon. Odysseus' heart beat faster with joy, and he did not even notice the clouds gathering over his raft, the wind getting up, or the sea growing choppy. And then, quite suddenly, the sky darkened all around him, and heavy clouds covered the sun. In no time Odysseus found himself in the centre of a violent storm, his little craft being smashed to bits. The sea grew angry, and tall waves tossed the raft to and fro like an eggshell.

This fury of the elements was the work of Poseidon, ruler of the oceans. When he found out that Odysseus had dared leave the island of Ogygia, he at once churned up the waves and veiled the sky with clouds.

"So that's how things are!" he ranted, furiously waving his trident, by means of which he could raise the sea swell and shake the land. "Those on Olympus have taken advantage of my absence to help Odysseus escape! The cunning King of Ithaca thinks the Phaeacians will help him! But it won't be as easy as he thinks! I'll give him a run for his money!"

And once more he raised the waves with his trident. Poor Odysseus was sure that his

last hour had come. Thoughts ran through his head as to how he might survive, while his raft leapt about on the waves like a paper toy. Would it not have been better, he thought, to have fallen at Troy, like so many of my valiant countrymen? At least I should have been granted the honour of a funeral, and should have been heralded for ever as a hero! Now I shall drown like a wretch and no one will so much as sigh at my passing.

At that moment a sudden wave caught his raft up in a whirlpool and turned it so roughly that the rudder was snatched from Odysseus' hands. A gust of wind snapped

the mast in two, and the yard and sail were blown into the sea. In an instant, Odysseus found himself under the waves; it was a wonder he was not killed by the rush of water. Only by a tremendous effort was he able to swim to the surface, where he managed to grab hold of his raft again.

But the storm raged on unabated. The winds blew angrily; the waves broke over the sorry remnants of the raft, and Odysseus was losing strength rapidly. Perhaps he would have perished, had not Leucothea, goddess of calm seas and patron of drowning sailors, caught sight of him at that moment. She flew down to him in the form of a seagull.

"What have you done to Poseidon, wretched human, that he should persecute you so? If you would escape his anger, leave your raft, take off your cloak, and wind this shawl around your breast. With it you can swim safely ashore — but when you get there, do not forget to unwind the shawl and to return it to me! If you throw it as far as you can out to sea, that will do."

And with these words the goddess vanished into the waves.

It was as if someone had poured new strength into Odysseus. He took one of the beams the raft was made of, sat astride it, took off the cloak Calypso had given him, and wrapped the goddess' shawl around his breast. Then he hurled himself into the sea once again and swam, with all the strength he could muster, in the direction in which he could see land.

Pallas Athene then hurried to help Odysseus. When Poseidon felt he had tormented Odysseus long enough, he climbed into his ocean chariot drawn by a team of horses with golden manes, and set off back to his palace beneath the waves. At that very moment Pallas bound the raging winds. Only one, Boreas, who was driving the waves towards the islands of the Phaeacians, was allowed to blow on, thus helping Odysseus on his way. Even so, he had to swim with all his might for two days and two nights before, at dawn on the third day, he at last saw dry land ahead.

But he was not yet out of danger. As he swam closer, he saw that the seashore consisted of huge, rocky cliffs, steep and inaccessible, against which the wailing and whining waves broke with a fearful din. He realised to his horror that they were driving him right into these cliffs, that either he would be smashed against them, or the waves would catch hold of him and hurl him back into the open sea. He tried to grab hold of one of the protruding rocks. For a while he hung on, until the mighty waves threw him against the rock face once more. His skin torn and bleeding, lashed by ever new onslaughts of rushing water and the stones which the sea drove along, Odysseus was rapidly losing his strength but eventually he managed to reach the mouth of a small stream which flowed into the sea.

Here at last was a place where he could swim ashore!

Odysseus crawled onto dry land; at that moment his legs gave way beneath him, and he collapsed, exhausted. He was covered in weals and scratches; sea water dripped from his nose and mouth, his body was caked with mud, and he could scarcely catch his

● ODYSSEUS IS FREED ●

61

breath. Almost instantly he fell into a deep faint.

When he came to his senses again, he recalled his promise to the goddess Leucothea. Unwinding her shawl, he staggered closer to the sea, and flung the cloth into the mouth of the stream, whose current carried it out to sea. He did not even see the kind goddess come to the surface to collect it, for he fell to his knees once more and devoutly kissed the rich soil upon which he had been saved. But what now?

If he were to spend the night on the banks of the river, how was he to survive the early morning cold, when he was already sapped of all his strength? And if he were to shelter in the forest somewhere, might he not be prey to wild beasts? How was he to defend himself in such a weak state?

As he looked around, he found a thicket of olive trees. One particular spot, he noticed, was protected from all sides by the trees. There was a thick carpet of fallen leaves, and Odysseus gathered them together to make a cosy bed. Then he lay down, covered himself with leaves, and curled up inside his lair.

Pallas Athene quickly closed his eyes, and Odysseus was overcome with exhaustion. He fell into a deep, refreshing sleep.

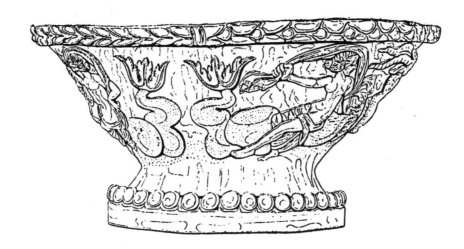

Nausicaa

Not far from Odysseus, in a richly ornamented chamber of the royal palace, there slept the beautiful daughter of Alcinous, king of the Phaeacians; her name was Nausicaa. Towards morning, her sleep was disturbed by a dream. Pallas Athene appeared, in the form of her dearest friend, inviting her to go down to the sea the next day, to the stream in the bay where they always did their washing together.

The dream was so lifelike that as soon as Nausicaa awoke in the morning she ran to ask her parents if she might go down to the sea. King Alcinous ordered the servants to make ready a cart with a wicker basket and harness mules to it, and her mother, Queen Arete, gave her food, wine and a golden jug of oil for the girls to rub onto themselves when the washing was done and they had bathed and wanted to sun themselves. Then the servants loaded the basket with Nausicaa's robes and the robes and garments of her mother, her father and her five brothers, until it was quite full. They took turns to drive it down to the stream where the girls did their washing.

They had plenty of work to do! They washed one piece after another, then soaked them in shallow pits in the sand, where they trod on them to get the dirt out; finally they laid them out on the pebbles by the shore to let the waves whiten them. In the meantime the girls bathed in the sea, rubbed themselves with oil, sat down, and waited for the washing to dry. Then Nausicaa had an idea — why not play with a ball? And she threw it at one of the servant-girls, who ducked out of the way; the ball fell into the water, and the girls all shrieked.

Their cries awoke the sleeping Odysseus. At first he started, wondering whose voices he could hear, but when he parted the bushes and saw the girls running about, he was reassured. He broke off a bushy branch from one of the shrubs and wound it around his body, so as not to show himself to them naked and stepped out of the thicket.

It was as if someone had fired an arrow into the midst of Nausicaa's companions. What was this fearful creature which had emerged? Its body was covered in cuts and bruises, its breast daubed with mud, and its hair filled with sea slime!

Only Princess Nausicaa stood still and looked Odysseus calmly in the eyes. He felt at first like throwing himself on his knees, crying out to her to clothe him and show him the way to human habitation; but he realised he might frighten or offend her. So he began to beg and flatter her:

"Noble lady, or goddess if so you be; I do not know who you are, but whoever you are, take pity on me! For twenty days a storm drove me across the ocean. I was lucky to escape with my life, but in the end I reached this piece of land from the island of Ogygia. I do not know where I am, nor am I acquainted with any living creature here. Show me, I beg of you, the way to the nearest city, and lend me a piece of cloth to hide my nakedness. I will be grateful for anything. And may the gods repay you; may they grant all your wishes — a good husband, a happy household, all that may bring you joy!"

"You speak quite finely, stranger," Nausicaa replied. "You seem neither evil nor foolish. Welcome to our land; you are on the island of Scheria, among the Phaeacians. I will be pleased to show you the way to the city, and have no fear that you will go unclothed. And that you may know to whom you are speaking, I am Nausicaa, daughter of the Phaeacian king, Alcinous."

She clapped her hands to call the servants.

"Why do you run away? Is this man you are so afraid of an enemy? Prepare him some food and drink, and take him somewhere where he may wash himself a little. And give him some clothes and a cloak, that he may show himself in the city."

The servant-girls obeyed. In a solitary spot Odysseus washed off the mud and slime, rubbed his body with oil, combed his thick hair, and donned clean clothes. When he returned from the shore to the group of girls, Nausicaa liked what she saw.

"See how it becomes the stranger — at first he looked like some spectre, striking terror into us, and now you would say he

was one of the happy ones who sit on Olympus. That would be a fine husband for me! Who knows, perhaps he will stay . . . And now, give him something to eat. Stranger, help yourself!"

Odysseus did not need asking twice, for had not eaten for a good while. He now did so greedily, gulping down lumps of food whole, and it was some time before he had eaten and drunk his fill. Then Nausicaa said:

"Now, stranger, we shall go to the city, to my father's palace. I will go first with the team, and show you the way. You shall follow with my servants on foot. But you may not enter the palace with us at once; you know how people's tongues wag. If they saw us together, they would say I had brought myself a husband, that none of the young men hereabouts is good enough for me. It would be better for you to stay outside the city in the grove of the goddess Athene. My father has vines there, and it is not far from there to the city walls — a mere stone's throw. Sit down there and wait a while, until I and the servants get home. Then set out for the walls and ask for the palace of my father, Alcinous. Any child will show you where it is. When you enter, cross the entrance hall quickly and make sure you get to the first chamber, where my mother receives visitors. She usually sits there by the hearth with her servants, leaning on a pillar. On the other side of her my father sits drinking wine. But speak to my mother first! If you can win her over, she will help you in all things."

With these words the graceful Nausicaa struck her team of mules with a gleaming whip, and off they went. She drove carefully, so that Odysseus and the servants might keep up with her.

The bright sun was sinking in the west when they reached the grove dedicated to the goddess Athene.

Nausicaa continued on her way without Odysseus.

He, meanwhile, sat among the aspen trees of the grove and turned his thoughts to his protectress, Pallas Athene. He begged her with all his heart to use her divine power to win the rulers of the Phaeacians over to him, to arouse in them sympathy and love for him. If only they would help him return to his homeland!

At the House of Alcinous

When the time appointed by Nausicaa had passed, Odysseus set out for the city. On the way he met a young girl who was carrying a jug of water, and as Nausicaa had advised him, asked the way to the palace of King Alcinous. He had no notion that he was speaking to Pallas Athene, who had taken that form in order to help him.

"You may go with me, stranger," said the girl. "I live with my father close to the royal palace, and we are going the same way."

Odysseus thanked her, not knowing that Pallas Athene had surrounded him with an impenetrable mist, so that none of the Phaeacians could see him. He set off after the unknown girl, and was filled with wonder. How imposing the city's buildings were! And how tall and strong the fortifications! And the harbour — how huge and elegant were the ships which anchored there!

At last they reached the royal palace, and Odysseus' guide took her leave of him with these words:

"We are here, stranger; you are standing before the royal palace. Go in boldly, but if you have something on your mind, I should advise you to win the favour of the queen. She is called Arete, and is highly regarded, like some goddess, for she is not only beautiful, but clever too. How often she has settled disputes of all kinds! She will surely help you!"

With these words she vanished.

Odysseus went inside the palace, and gazed in wonder at the splendour he found there. He entered through golden gates set in a silver frame and guarded by golden and silver dogs beaten out by Hephaestus himself, the god of fire. The walls of the chambers were of copper, and in the banqueting hall there stood two rows of seats covered with rare drapes, beside which stood the figures of boys made of pure gold.

In their hands torches blazed, lighting up the entire hall.

Odysseus passed through the chambers, protected by the mist with which Pallas Athene had surrounded him, until he reached the banqueting hall. The noble Phaeacians and King Alcinous himself were at that very moment drinking a toast to the keen-sighted god Hermes. But Odysseus passed by them, making straight for the throne of Queen Arete, where he threw himself at her feet. The protective mist which had surrounded him melted away, and suddenly the royal company saw an unknown man kneeling before the queen's throne.

"Arete, most noble lady," Odysseus said plaintively, "I kneel as a suppliant at your feet, have recourse to you and your spouse, adjure you both: take pity on me, and extend to me a helping hand. For many years I have wandered the world, suffered the most fearful tribulations, and now a dreadful storm has cast me up on the shores of your island. Help me to fulfil my dearest desire — to get back to my homeland as quickly as possible."

For a moment all were left speechless.

They surveyed in silence this plaintively pleading stranger of noble countenance, until at last the oldest of the Phaeacian noblemen broke the tense silence.

"Alcinous, it is neither pleasant nor polite to allow this stranger to kneel thus before us. All seem to be waiting to see what you have to say, so you should tell him to take a seat. And he should be given a cup of wine, so that we may all drink to the ruler of thunder, the mighty Zeus."

Alcinous seemed to have been waiting for these words. He took Odysseus by the hand, raised him up from the ground, and led him to the seat beside his throne where his favourite son Laodamas was wont to sit. Then, at a signal from the king, a servant-girl brought a beautiful golden jug filled with water, and Odysseus washed his hands over a silver bowl. The keeper of the royal larder placed bread on the table, and a page filled everyone's cup with wine. They poured away a few drops in honour of the gods, and then drank a toast among themselves.

At last Alcinous said:

"Noble Phaeacians, we cannot remain deaf to a plea such as that we have just heard. Listen to what I propose: that in the morning we meet again. We shall invite the elders of the community, too, then play host to the stranger, and offer sacrifices to the gods. We shall do all that is in our power to help our guest return home. We shall see to it that he makes the journey, and what awaits him when he gets there has long ago been decided by the fates, on the day he came into the world. Unless he himself is one of the immortal Olympians, who visit us from time to time in human guise."

"Dismiss this thought from your mind, my lord," replied Odysseus. "I, one of the divinities from Olympus? No, I am an ordinary mortal, who has suffered more than enough at the hands of the gods! And though it is surely no easy task for me to reach my home, I desire nothing more than to return there."

Then Queen Arete, too, addressed Odysseus. She had noted the cloak and the

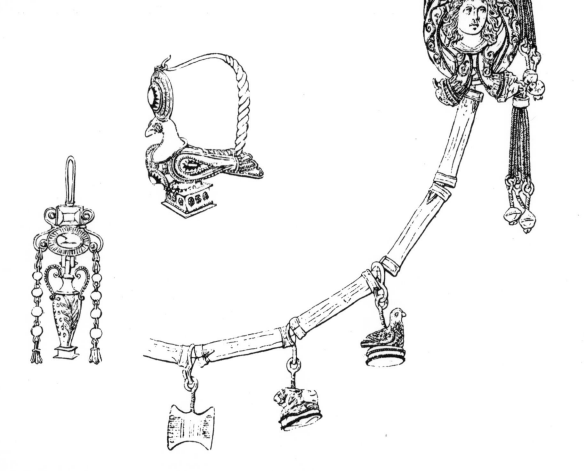

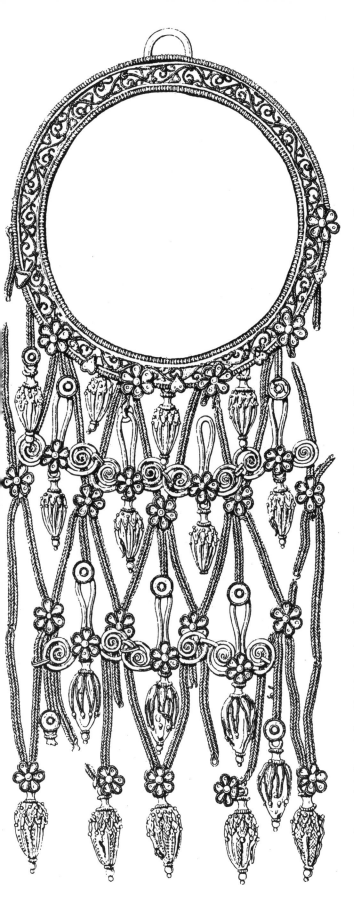

robes Nausicaa had given him (for had she not woven them herself with her servants?), and wondered how he had come by them.

"May I ask you something?" she said. "Who are, you, dear guest? And how is it that you are dressed so finely? Did you not tell us that you were washed up on our shores after long wanderings by a storm?"

"It would be a long story indeed, were I to tell everything I have endured up to this moment, O queen," Odysseus replied with a sigh. "I should have to tell how, as I sailed across the open sea, Zeus smashed my craft to a thousand pieces with his lightning. How I floated on what was left of the keel to the island of Ogygia. And also how I was offered shelter by Calypso, a beautiful nymph, and how she tried to persuade me to take her as my wife, promising me immortality and eternal youth. When, after eight years, she released me, for seventeen days I sailed the ocean, before I sighted on the horizon the shores of the isle of Scheria. But the ruler of the seas, Poseidon, let loose a gale and stirred up the surface of the waters, and I only managed to escape the clutches of the elements and reach the dry land of Scheria with the last of my strength. In a thicket, buried beneath fallen leaves, I slept through the night, morning and noon. It was not until late in the afternoon that I was awoken by cries, and spied a group of girls playing by the sea shore. Among them was your own daughter, O queen, the noble Nausicaa. It was she who gave me these splendid clothes, and looked after me. Your daughter has a sensitive, noble heart!"

The queen liked Odysseus' words, but Alcinous was none too pleased.

"My daughter did not act very wisely," he

objected. "If you asked her for help, she should have brought you straight here."

"Do not chide her for it, my lord," Odysseus begged. "It was I who did not wish it to be so. I was afraid you might be angry, were she to come here with a strange man."

"I should not be angry, were you to explain everything as you have done now. I am pleased to see the likes of you, and should like to have such a son-in-law, upon whom I should heap riches. But I know it cannot be so. You long to return home, and no Phaeacian may prevent you. We will not delay. You shall rest, and tomorrow we will take you to your homeland. You shall see what fine mariners the Phaeacians are! And now, it is time to sleep."

Odysseus thanked the king warmly, and Queen Arete herself saw to it that the servants prepared a bed for their guest in the palace arcade. They laid down beautiful red drapes, on which they placed woollen blankets, and then by torchlight put the exhausted Odysseus in his carved wooden bed. After so many arduous days he fell sound asleep again in no time at all . . .

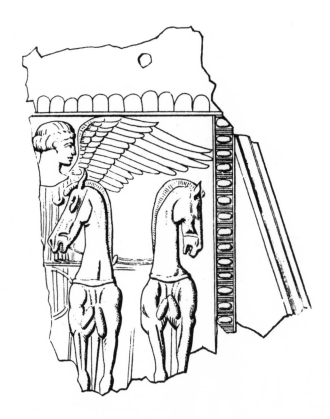

The Song of Demodocus

The next day the king ordered fifty-two of the best Phaeacian sailors to prepare a good ship and to provide it with all that was required for a long voyage. He told the leaders of the Phaeacian people of his decision, and invited all of them, great captains and noblemen, young and revered elders, to a banquet in the royal palace.

And what a feast it was! Alcinous ordered two cows, eight pigs and twelve sheep to be slaughtered, and fine wines to be brought for all. When they had eaten and drunk their fill, the blind singer Demodocus took up his lute and began to sing a moving song of heroism.

And what was that song about, that the Phaeacians listened to so intently?

What were the events which so captivated them that they all trembled, now with horror, now with emotion? That they sometimes clenched their fists, sometimes clutched at their throats, or laid their hands on their temples?

The voice of blind Demodocus rang out, one moment full of sadness, the next stormy, as he began to tell the tale of the

fearful wrath of Achilles, boldest of those who had set out to punish the seducer Paris, and to tear away from him the beautiful Helen, whom he had abducted.

"It was the tenth year of the Achaeans' siege of Troy," sang Demodocus, "and there came the unhappy moment when Agamemnon grievously offended Achilles. And then the thrice more unfortunate one when Achilles declared in response that they would no longer see either him or his best friend, Patroclus, on the battlefield. They were soon to see the significance of his decision. When the Trojans, led by Hector, rushed out from the city, they so shook the Greek ranks, lacking the example of Achilles, that the besieging army was driven back almost to the place where the Achaean ships were anchored. Agamemnon was desperate, and did not know what to do. He

sent envoys to Achilles, with Odysseus at their head. The Ithacan king had many times shown his ingenuity and eloquence; nor did he disappoint his fellows this time. He managed at least to persuade the insulted Achilles to lend Patroclus his armour, which the defenders of Troy knew so well. Perhaps Patroclus, wearing the armour, could save the Greeks from defeat!

"They made ready a chariot, harnessing Achilles' swift horses to it, and Patroclus took his place at the head of the Greek army. The moment the Trojans spotted him, they were inspired with fear, and took flight, shouting: 'The invulnerable Achilles has returned to the battlefield!' Only a handful of the bravest had the courage to stay in front of the battlements.

"And now Hector, encouraged by the god Apollo, was riding forth to do battle with Patroclus. He hurled a stone at his charioteer, and when the latter fell from the chariot, the two warriors were left face to face. Hector grasped Patroclus by the head, while the Greek hero gripped his adversary by the legs, as if he were holding him in a pair of pincers. Then Patroclus, amid the fearful carnage, which had been unleashed on all sides, with unimaginable ferocity, was struck in the back by a lance. Apollo, patron of the Trojans, had come down from the ramparts veiled in a cloud, and entered the fray to help Hector. He threw down Patroclus' helm, which rolled beneath the horses' hooves with a loud clanging, tore away his shield, and loosened his armour. Then

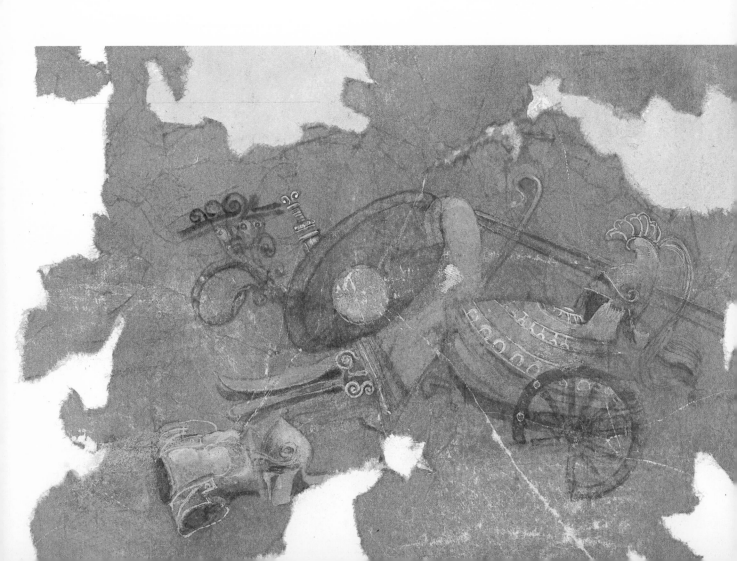

Hector drove his sword into Achilles' friend.

"At once a fierce struggle broke out for Patroclus' lifeless body. It seemed as if the Trojans would drag it off as booty, when Achilles, who had heard of his friend's death, appeared on the battlefield. Three times he roared so terribly that the Trojans were terror-stricken, and panicked. Then the Greeks were able to carry back the body of their hero; Achilles wept over it all night long, and swore he would not allow him to be buried before he had dragged there the one who had slain him, and killed a dozen Trojans in revenge.

"The next morning Achilles' mother, Thetis, brought him new armour, fashioned of gold in the forge of Hephaestus himself, god of fire and armourer of the gods. When the Greek hero put it on, he looked even more terrible then before. Then Agamemnon took back his insults in front of the assembled army, and the Greeks charged into battle once again. The ringing of weapons was again heard on the plain which stretched out in front of Troy; the ground shook beneath the pounding of horses' hooves, and the roar of the war chariots sounded like Zeus' own thunder. Again a fierce battle was joined. Achilles fought like a lion, spreading terror all around him. He drove most of the Trojan army back to the River Xanthus, and so many warriors fell to blows from his sword that they blocked the flow of the water.

"Just as the Trojan warriors were wavering, and began to retreat in order to seek the safety of their ramparts, Hector appeared beneath the city gates, resolved to meet Achilles in a battle of life and death. It was in vain that his father Priam implored him not to do battle with a hero who had already sent so many Trojans to the grim underworld realm of the god Hades. At the last instant Hector's courage left him: three times he was chased around the city walls, but failed to find shelter, or to take refuge inside the gates. Achilles always cut off his retreat. Before the eyes of the desperate King Priam he caught up with the Trojan hero and drove his lance through him. Then he tied his enemy's body to his chariot by the feet, triumphantly dragged it around the city walls, and hauled it back to the Greek camp.

"That very same night King Priam himself visited Achilles, heaping upon him offers of a ransom for his son's body, and heart-rending pleas that he return it. He appealed to the victor's sympathy, imploring him to return the body of his dearest son, so that he might be given a dignified funeral. Achilles was overcome with emotion: Priam had lost his dearest son, he his best-loved friend. In an instant charged with feeling, when tears were streaming down both their faces, Achilles relented. He had Hector's body rubbed with fragrant oil, gave orders for it to be wrapped in a beautiful shroud, and what was more promised that for twelve days, until the funeral ceremonies were over, the Greeks would observe a truce.

"But before long Achilles himself was to meet his fate. Again the fighting raged, again the brave Achilles met the defenders of Troy in cruel encounters, until the day came when Paris' arrow struck him in the heel, the only vulnerable spot on his body. For seventeen days and nights the Greeks mourned their greatest hero, until they placed his remains alongside Patroclus' ashes

and raised a noble tumulus over them.

"And again the Greeks began to argue. Who was to inherit Achilles' golden armour? The boldest? The most deserving? But who was it to be? Ajax, who had saved Achilles' body, dragging it from the tumult of battle, or Odysseus, who had persuaded the Greeks to fight on when they wanted to sail for home, and who had by his cunning seized the Trojans' rare horses from their camp? Agamemnon and Menelaus awarded the golden armour to Odysseus, and thus cruelly offended Ajax. He took their decision as an insult which could only be wiped out by blood . . ."

And Demodocus continued his song.

"Not even Odysseus kept Achilles' armour for long, for he knew he must give it, though with a heavy heart, to Achilles' son. A prophesy had stated that the Greeks

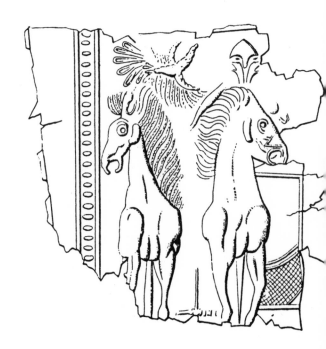

would not enter the gates of Troy as victors until Achilles' son stood in their ranks in his father's armour. So once more Odysseus bowed to the words of a prophesy. It had after all, been foretold that the Greeks would not conquer Troy while Pallas Athene's statue stood in her temple, the one which Zeus himself had flung down from Olympus to mark the place where Troy was to stand. Odysseus, dressed as a beggar, had seized it boldly. And perhaps it was at that moment, when he carried off the sacred statue, that he had the idea which decided the whole thing, which brought destruction to the city, death to Priam, doom on his descendants, grief to all mothers, booty to the victors, laurels to Odysseus, Helen to Menelaus; which caused that to come about which Zeus had wanted from the first."

Demodocus finished his song, and the

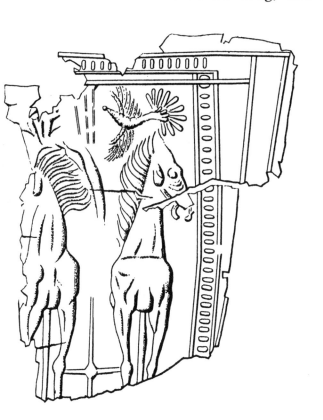

tense atmosphere began to ease. All those who had listened to the tales of heroic deeds, of the spite of gods and men, of magnanimous sacrifice and petty ambition, slowly began to relax as the scenes of cruel warfare vanished from their eyes. At last they saw before them not the blood-soaked plains outside the walls of Troy, but the ornamented banqueting hall, and cups brimming with fine wine.

But how bitter and heart-rending was Demodocus' song to the ears of Odysseus! He felt as though he were standing once more outside the gates of Troy, as if he could hear again the cries of his comrades, the groans of wounded horses, the clash of arms in the middle of the night, in that final battle with the enemy. And he had to hide his head in his cloak, so that no one might see the salty tears running down his cheeks.

Yet Alcinous did not fail to notice — for his guest was again sitting right beside him in the seat where his beloved son Laodamas usually sat. When he heard Odysseus sigh and sob, he wished to tear him from his sorrow. He stood up, clapped his hands three times, and said:

"Noble Phaeacians; we have refreshed ourselves with good food, and we have heard Demodocus' lute — now we should spend some time in games and contests! Let us see who is the strongest wrestler, who can run fastest, and who can throw the discus furthest! Our guest will surely be interested, and will tell his friends of our excellent performances!"

The Phaeacians were enthusiastic at this suggestion. Everyone rushed to the arena; everyone was anxious to see the best of Phaeacian youth.

The contests were excellent. When the king's favourite son, Laodamas, beat all his rivals in the fist-fighting contest, he challenged Odysseus to show what he could do. Did not physical fitness, agility and strength belong to every true man?

But Odysseus hesitated.

"My dear Laodamas," he objected, "I have no thought for competition. I do not yet feel well after my sufferings, and in spirit I am already at sea and on my way home."

Laodamas would have satisfied himself with this reply, but the winner of the wrestling match, drunk with his own success, began to mock Odysseus.

"Are these not mere excuses, stranger? Who knows if you are capable of such things as throwing the discus! Or if you are not just one of those traders who roam the seas, and are interested in nothing more than the quickest way to fill their purses?"

These words angered Odysseus.

"You hold your nose a little too high, my friend," he said with annoyance. "I see that the gods have given you a good figure and a handsome face, but not too many brains. You do not seem to know that modesty is a part of even the greatest of men. Am I to recount how many I have defeated in the past? I am not in good form, but you shall see what I am capable of!"

And just as he was, without removing his cloak, he grabbed a discus, the biggest of them all, spun round several times, and hurled it high above the heads of the watching Phaeacians. The discus whistled through the air and landed on the ground in the distance, further than any of the competitors had thrown.

The sneering wrestler looked crestfallen; the crowd murmured its admiration, and Alcinous himself apologised to Odysseus.

"I trust you will not take offence at the wrestler's jibes. At least you have convinced us that you are a real man. Not only are you clever, but a good sportsman, too. Let us return to the palace! We will listen to Demodocus again."

The feast continued. This time the great singer entertained them with a sprightly song about love and Odysseus liked it very much this time, and praised it in front of them all. Then he congratulated the dancers, saying that never before had he seen anyone dance so beautifully.

When the young Phaeacians had finished dancing, Alcinous called upon twelve of the noblest captains to have gifts brought for Odysseus.

Odysseus received from each of them a fine robe for his journey, together with a coin of pure gold. Queen Arete offered him a beautiful chest, and King Alcinous a magnificent golden cup, that he might have something by which to remember the king of the Phaeacians whenever he offered a sacrifice to Zeus and the other gods. As a token of reconciliation, the wrestler brought Odysseus a bronze sword with a silver handle and a sheath of carved ivory.

Princess Nausicaa also came to take her leave of him.

"They say you are leaving for home already, dear guest — then may you enjoy good health, and never forget me when you reach your homeland. Perhaps I have helped you just a little in this . . ."

"Beautiful Nausicaa," Odysseus replied, overcome with emotion, "may you be right that I shall soon be home. And you, dear

lady, I shall never forget; day by day I will recall how kind you have been to me. Without you I should surely have perished."

The servant-girls washed Odysseus and rubbed his body with fragrant oil, packing his gifts into the beautiful chest he had been given by Queen Arete. Then they all met at table one last time to say farewell. When Demodocus was again led into the hall, Odysseus cut a piece of meat from the roast boar with his own hands to offer the blind singer, as a mark of respect.

"Demodocus, you have a talent given by the gods themselves; I daresay Apollo himself must have been your teacher," he said with admiration. "Whether you are telling a tale or singing of anything at all, it is always as if you had lived through it yourself. You sang to us of the battles outside the walls of Troy. Now sing of how the Greeks built a wooden horse, and how Odysseus and the boldest of the warriors had hidden inside it!"

Demodocus did as Odysseus asked.

As he sang, the King of Ithaca recalled once more all he had lived through long ago, saw in front of him those events long past; and again he was overcome with emotion, until Alcinous had once more to stop the great Demodocus from singing.

"Friends, I know you like Demodocus' song; but let him not continue. At a banquet all should rejoice, yet our guest only sighs, and sighs. If there is some weight on your mind, my friend, then tell us all about it. And tell us at last what your name is, where your home is, where our swift vessels are to carry you. Why do you lament so whenever the battles for Troy are mentioned? Did one of your relatives die there? Or a friend, whom you loved above all others on earth? Tell us!"

"Mighty and renowned Alcinous," Odysseus replied, "I suppose I have spoilt your entertainment and that of the others; if so, I am sorry for it. And I understand that you wish to know what lies behind it, and who I am. Very well. In gratitude for the way you have received me, I will tell you all. I am that Odysseus who had the wooden horse built before the gates of Troy; I am Laertes' son, ruler of the island of Ithaca, the sweetest corner of this earth I know. You will also hear of all the places in this world where I have wandered. But, however beautiful they were, or however lovely the women who tried to win me, I could never forget Ithaca, or Penelope, or my son Telemachus. For ten years I took part in the siege of Troy. Demodocus has sung to you of the fall of that great city. From me you shall hear all the things that Zeus made us suffer on our journey home from Troy . . ."

And Odysseus began his story.

The Cicones and the Lotus-eaters

"You have heard, my lord, and you, too, my lady, of our heroic deeds, and of the battles fought by the Achaean Greeks," Odysseus began. "When at last we had taken the city of Troy and destroyed Priam's proud castle, the gods sowed discord and dissension in our ranks. After that war we all wanted to return home, but some wanted to leave at once, while others wished to wait and hold a sacrificial ceremony to the gods. Menelaus wanted to depart as soon as possible; after all, he had regained his beautiful wife Helen. But Agamemnon thought the army should stay in Troy. Not long before all had been united in their will to destroy the city, but the moment the enemy was subdued, strife broke out between the supporters of the two kings. For a day and a night we held a council that was to decide the matter. But neither side was prepared to give way; ill feeling began to spread, and each group suspected the other of the worst intentions. So half of us stayed behind with Agamemnon, while half sailed away on swift ships with Menelaus.

"It was an ill-starred voyage, though the ocean was kind to us at first. By and by the wind blew my twelve ships to Ismarus, the city of the Cicones, where we disembarked. We took rich booty there, dividing it between us fairly, and I was in favour of setting out again at once. If only my companions had listened to me! If only they had not been so sure that they were in no danger there! But they wished to celebrate their victory with wine and roast meats, not suspecting that those we had defeated had called upon their countrymen inland to come to their aid. Our camp by the shore was attacked by overwhelming numbers of them. There were more Cicones than flowers and leaves in the springtime; they

came with chariots, and were more than well armed. Though we fought bravely, it was all we could do to beat off their attack and retreat to our ships. That afternoon we counted our losses: seventy-two of my companions lost their lives in the battle with the Cicones, six from every ship . . .

"For nine days we were driven across the seas. Shortly after our escape from Ismarus, we were surprised by a cold north wind, which gave our sails a good shake out. Only then did the sea calm down slightly, and we were able to rest a little at least.

"We mended our sails, set them again, and on the tenth day reached land once more. We wanted to take on water for our journey, and so I sent three of my companions to find out the lie of the land.

"For a long time there was no sign of my scouts — so long that I decided in the end to go and seek them myself. I went deeper and deeper inland. All around as far as the eye could see were the blue and white flowers of lotus blossoms. Now, I thought, I knew why my friends had not returned.

"We were in the land of the Lotus-eaters!

"I was sized with horror and anxiety.

"Those peculiar people behaved towards strangers in a friendly manner, offering their hospitality to all — but they always offered the food which they ate themselves, lotus blossom. They know how to make an

● THE CICONES AND THE LOTUS-EATERS ●

excellent, tasty dish of it, but he who once eats it forgets all he has lived through before — homeland, mother, children; he never more wishes to return home, and wants to stay with the Lotus-eaters for ever.

"And that was what had happened to my companions. They would not hear of returning to the ship; all my persuasion was in vain. I had to bind them and carry them off by force, and place them below decks in bonds. They lamented and wept as though we had wronged them terribly.

"I convinced the others that it would be dangerous to stay in those parts any longer; I was afraid that others, perhaps out of curiosity, might wish to try the food of the Lotus-eaters, and thus fall under the spell of forgetfulness.

"One by one our ships, with their red-painted prows, left that quiet bay, and their swift oars churned up the surface of the water, taking us back to the open sea. We were despondent, tormented by anxieties; nor had we any notion of what awaited us in the land of the wild and arrogant Cyclops."

The Cave of Polyphemus

"When we anchored," continued Odysseus, "everything was as black as pitch. Thick, heavy clouds blotted out every last ray of moonlight, and Zeus himself must have guided us, for we could not see more than ten paces ahead! It was not until morning, when rosy Eos lit up the sky, that we saw how fate had led us into a calm anchorage. It offered our ships good protection from wind and waves, and what was more, herds of goats were grazing on the slopes around us. We only had to take up our bows and arrows, and we would have food enough.

"Our bag was a rich one — nine goats for each ship. We made fires and cooked the tasty meat, quenching our thirst with the wine we had seized from the Cicones. There was also a clear spring which flowed at the end of the bay. As we feasted, we had noticed that on the far side, across the bay from where we were, there was another island. We could hear the bleating of sheep and goats and the sound of unknown voices, and we could see smoke rising skywards, and the flames of a fire.

"I did not yet know that the sea had

carried us to the island of the Cyclops, those foolish, lazy and malevolent creatures who instead of houses live in lairs and caves. They cultivate nothing and have no skills. They know nothing of grafting fruit trees, tilling the soil or growing vines! They live like a dumb people. They cannot build either a house or a boat, or put together the simplest of carts. They rely entirely on what the land offers them. But the soil is so fertile there that the fields produce barley without ploughing; on the slopes vines are heavy with juicy grapes, the vast meadows provide pasture for countless flocks of sheep and goats, and the branches of trees are covered in fruit.

"I was persuaded to explore the island which we could see. Early in the morning I left our bay and rowed with my crew to the opposite shore. The wind was against us, and we had to lean hard on the oars, but nonetheless the trip did not take us long.

"The first thing we saw was a strip of dense forest. Huge oak trees and firs grew there, and in one place, not far from the shore, we could see a large cave. It was wound round with creeping laurel, and there was a wide open space in front of it, walled on all sides with huge boulders set firmly into the ground. It seemed that someone lived there, but what a giant he must be, a huge fellow, a colossus of immense size!

"I chose the twelve boldest members of the crew (while the others stayed to guard the ship), telling them to bring along wine to quench our thirst, and we set off together to scout. We climbed over the wall of boulders without coming across anyone. We entered the cave without difficulty. But as soon as we stepped inside we stood amazed. All around

the lair, which was the size of several houses, we saw stacks of food, as far as the eye could see: great yellow cheeses stood in baskets; white sheep's whey filled milking pails and buckets; stalls and pens were crammed with lambs and kids, the older ones, the middle ones and those born latest being kept separately.

"My companions stared in wonder. They wanted to take what cheese we could carry and make off with it; some wanted to take along the oldest of the lambs at least; but I was deaf and dumb to their proposals. I wanted to know who lived in that cave, at least to catch sight of this strange creature with my own eyes. I expected him to greet us cordially and perhaps to make us a gift of something. In other words, I did not want to leave. So we sat there, cutting off pieces of cheese to taste, and waiting for the stranger to return.

"It was evening by the time he came back from pasture. On his back he carried a huge load of dry wood, and when he dropped it in the cave, it made such a din that we leapt up in terror and crouched in a corner of the cave.

"For a while we were not able to see him properly. Only gradually were we able to make out an enormous mass of flesh, a hairy body, arms like oak trees, a face like a square boulder, and in the middle of its forehead a single, evil, gleaming eye.

"The giant drove all the sheep and goats he had brought from pasture into his lair, and rolled across the doorway a stone so huge that not even a team of horses could have shifted it. Then he sat down and began to milk the sheep and goats; he did it well, like a skilled shepherd. He left half the milk

to curdle for cheese, and poured the other half into vessels from which he might drink it. When he had finished, he lit a fire, looked around the cave, and saw us crouching in the corner of his lair.

"When he spoke to us, it was like the rolling of thunder.

"'What have we here? Guests, I see! Where have you come from? You have come by the wet route? Have you some business here? Or are you pirates, on the look-out for ships?'

"'We are ... Achaeans ... fighting Greeks ... we were driven ... here ... by a storm ... we are returning ... from distant ... Troy ... we belong ... to the army ... of King Agamemnon ... now we want ... to go home ... we are lost ... if you might offer us ... your hospitality ... for the gods ... Zeus himself ... decree that ... one should help ... those who wander.'

"'So the gods decree, do they! Zeus himself, eh! Don't give me that nonsense! I am not afraid of your gods. We are the Cyclops; we are stronger than any Zeus, and I am the strongest of all, Polyphemus. You would do better to tell me where your ship lies.'

"'Poseidon has destroyed it,' I lied, quickly. 'It was smashed to bits against the cliffs when we were landing. Only I and my twelve companions were saved.'

"Polyphemus said nothing to this, but all at once he reached out one of his huge arms and grabbed two of my companions. He struck them several times against the rocks, and we watched with horror as he broke their bones, tore off their limbs, and stuffed them down his horrible throat.

"He swallowed large lumps, smacking his lips with satisfaction, and washed each one down with a large swig of goat's milk. Then he lay down among his sheep and goats, closed his one eye, and started to snore.

"At first I felt like hurling myself upon him and sinking my sword to the hilt in his groin, but I came to my senses in time. What about the huge boulder at the mouth of the cave? Who would roll it away for us? Those of us who were left could not move it an inch, and to stay in the cave would mean dying a slow and horrible death. All night long I worried how we might save ourselves . . .

"In the morning the Cyclops awoke, and another two of us paid for his appetite with their lives. Then he rolled the stone back from the doorway, drove out his sheep and goats, and put it back in place, leaving us with the melancholy thought of who his victims would be at suppertime. We were imprisoned in his lair as in a trap, and no one had any idea how to escape the clutches of Polyphemus. It was only when I explored the cave, hoping desperately to find a way out, that I noticed a huge stake, the size of a ship's mast or a tree trunk, in the sheep pen. Suddenly, I had an idea.

"In the evening, when the one-eyed fellow returned, we were ready. The huge stake was sharpened to a point at one end, hardened in a fire, and hidden beneath the glowing ashes in a corner of the cave. The giant did as he had the day before. He rolled back the boulder, let in the sheep and goats, then entered the cave and rolled the stone back into place. When he had finished his milking, he looked us over, and chose two of us for supper.

"Summoning all my strength, I poured the wine from the skin we had with us into one of the troughs, and stepped forward to face Polyphemus.

"'Cyclops, since you know what human flesh tastes like, you should try our wine,' I said. 'It is excellent, the last drop we rescued from the ship. Perhaps when you have drunk you will take pity on us and not be so cruel.'

"The Cyclops said nothing, but he emptied the trough in one gulp and belched contentedly.

"'Your wine is not so bad; we have none like that here. In return for it you will receive a gift from me. Pour me some more, and tell me your name.'

"I poured him out some more, and the Cyclops emptied the trough as if it were a thimble, then wanted another, and another. The wine was slowly going to his head.

"'What is your name, then?' he blabbered, slurring his words.

"'*Nobody*, Cyclops, since you wish to know,' I said. '*Nobody* is my name. But what gift shall I receive from you?'

"His head was swaying to and fro, and he fixed me drunkenly with his one eye.

"'You gave me very good wine, Nobody,' he blurted. 'Did I say I should give you a present? Then, Nobody, in return for your wine I will eat you last of all. I will eat all of you, but you, Nobody . . . right . . . at . . . the . . . end. Now . . . Nobody . . . I am — going . . . to sleep.'

"He fell over backwards and lay senseless in the middle of his lair. From the corner of his mouth the last swig of wine dribbled out, and then came a great snoring, like when

lava starts to pour from a volcano, and Polyphemus was fast asleep.

"Now our moment had come at last!

"I signalled to my companions, and we held the point of our stake over the licking flames of the fire, and waited for it to catch fire. Then, heaving together, we raised it up high and brought it down with all our might into the sleeping giant's eye. It hissed as when a blacksmith quenches hot iron, and the Cyclops gave out such a cry that the whole cave shook as if in an earthquake. He felt for the stake, pulled it out of his eye, and threw it aside. Quickly, we jumped out of the way. The giant began to move around the cave, lashing out on all sides with his hands, and roaring so loudly that the other Cyclops from all around gathered outside his lair.

" 'What is it? Why are you making such a noise, Polyphemus? Why do you wake us? Is someone stealing your sheep?' voices came from outside. But Polyphemus ran around the cave and shouted at the top of his voice:

" 'Nobody! Friends — Nobody!'

" 'Then why are you making such a fuss and shouting, as if you were being roasted on a spit? Is anyone slaying you?'

" 'How can you ask?' cried Polyphemus, mad with pain. 'Nobody! Don't you understand — No — body!'

" 'You've had too much to drink again,' the Cyclops replied from outside, and I trembled with satisfaction at the way my cleverly invented name had confounded them. 'You had no need to wake us up, and if you are so confused in the head, then you should pray to your father, Poseidon!'

" 'Wait! Don't go! He is here, the

scoundrel! The wretch! I'll catch him, though!' Polyphemus raged on.

" 'Catch whom? Who is there?'

" 'Nobody! Nobody!' Polyphemus repeated stubbornly, until the Cyclops waved their hands and went back to their rocky homes. They could be heard to say: he's had too much to drink, or else he's gone mad; then the voices grew fainter, and in the end could be heard no longer.

"For a while Polyphemus still ran about the cave, feeling in every corner, but then, when he couldn't find us, he sat down by the entrance and stretched out his arms. Perhaps he thought we should try to slip out, and that then he would catch us. But I was not such a fool as to run straight into his arms! Now, when I knew well enough how we should get the better of him!

"That evening Polyphemus had let into the cave rams as well as sheep, and they were fine, fat animals with thick, dark wool. The cave was full of them. It was clear that the giant would let them out to pasture again in the morning, and I hit on an idea. When the Cyclops had calmed down a little, we took some of the willow switches which were lying all around the cave, drove the rams into a bunch, and began to tie them together in threes. Beneath the middle one we tied one of our men, burying him well into the wool. It was so thick that they were lost among it, and anyway they were protected by the other rams at the side. Then I chose a particularly large animal, which was surely the biggest of the whole flock, and hung from his belly, curling up and pressing against him. Then I waited with patience and resolve for Eos to light the morning sky.

"Polyphemus began to let the herd out to pasture early in the morning. The wound in his eye must have hurt him a great deal, for he had moaned and groaned all night long, and even now, as he sat beside the boulder at the entrance to the cave, he kept whining with pain. But he was careful to see that we did not escape. He let the animals out one by one, and felt each of them carefully all along their backs from head to tail and then back again.

"All along their backs! And in the meantime we, pressed to their bellies from underneath, and, I must admit, at that moment quite terrified, escaped one by one from the cave. As he let out the last animal, the biggest of the rams, to which I was clinging, a sigh escaped his hairy chest.

"'You're the last? Usually you're out in front of the flock — but then I daresay you feel sorry for your master today. If only you could help me! But you would have to be able to speak, and tell me where that rascal who caused me such pain has hidden himself! Nobody! If only I could get hold of him I should squash him to pulp! How I should enjoy eating him!' Then he slapped the ram on the back and let him go. And

I and all my companions were safely out of the cave.

"For a while we stayed hidden beneath the rams' bellies, but as soon as the flock was some distance away from Polyphemus' cave, I let myself down and ran to untie the others. Our joy was spoilt only by the thought of our six companions who had not returned. Quickly, we prepared to set sail.

"As we were leaving the bay, we saw Polyphemus staggering across the hillside, finding his way from memory from his cave down to the shore. I could not resist cupping my hands to my mouth.

"'Cyclops Polyphemus,' I called, 'you got what you deserved! You thought you were faced with cowards, and wanted to end our lives. Now you have been punished!'

"He recognised my voice at once.

"With a howl that nearly deafened those aboard our ship, he tore a lump of rock off the cliff face above his cave and hurled this gigantic boulder, the size of half a hill, in the direction of our vessel. It fell in the water astern of us, nearly smashing the rudder; a mighty whirlpool formed where it landed, threatening to draw the ship back towards the island.

"'Lean on your oars, quickly, or we shall be sucked back again!' I shouted to my fellows, who were gaping in horror at the huge figure of the enraged Cyclops.

"They came to their senses and pulled with all their might, and the ship surged forward towards the open sea.

"'Do not taunt him, Odysseus,' they called to me, seeing me run to the ship's side, 'or he will throw the whole hill at us and sink our ship.'

"But at that moment I was beside myself

with malicious joy over the way we had managed to give Polyphemus the slip. Moreover I was fearfully angry that six of my men had lost their lives in his cave, so I kept on mocking him, like one possessed.

" 'We fooled you, Polyphemus! And if anyone should ask who the Nobody was who gave you good wine and whom you wished to honour with your shameful gift, it was Odysseus, King of Ithaca, renowned warrior at Troy, son of King Laertes. That is the truth of it, you one-eyed blind man.'

" 'What is that you say — you are Odysseus?' the Cyclops howled. 'Then the baneful prophesy has been fulfilled, which said that I should lose my sight when the Ithacan hero came! But how was I to know that it would be such a tiny fellow? That he would think up such a trick with wine and a false name? Wait, Odysseus; come back! I must tell you something! My father is the god Poseidon. He will heal my eye again; come back, I will ask him to give you a safe voyage, you will see!'

"'I should have to be crazy,' I called to him. 'I'll never fall for that one, Cyclops!'

"At that the terrible giant gritted his teeth, raised his hands to heaven and began to call upon the ruler of the seas, Poseidon, who with his trident stirs up the waters and shakes the land.

" 'Can you hear me, father? Odysseus has taken away my sight! Avenge me, and never allow him to return home safely! And if fate has decreed that he shall touch his native soil again, then let him stagger onto it as a poor beggar, alone, from a stranger's ship; may he not find a single stone of his home!'

"And again he broke off a huge piece of rock, much bigger than the first and, swinging it round his head, he hurled it at our ship. It crashed into the sea just astern of the rudder, almost smashing it to bits. Once again the sea splashed high into the air, the waves it raised lifting our craft right up, but fortunately setting it down near where the other ships rode at anchor.

"At last we could be sure we had escaped Polyphemus. The first thing I did was to thank Zeus for his protection. I chose the biggest and fattest ram from the herd we had captured, and offered it as a sacrifice to him.

"But Zeus did not accept my offering as I was soon to discover."

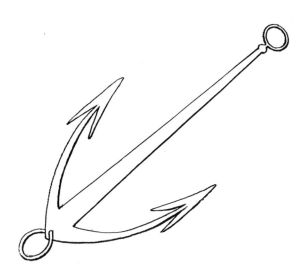

A Gift from the Wind God

"At first everything went well," Odysseus continued his story to the Phaeacians.

"When we left the Cyclops' Island of Goats, we headed in the direction of Ithaca, and after several days reached a floating island, enclosed by metal walls.

"It was the home of the wind god, Aeolus, who lives there in a palace on a tall rock and devotes himself with his six sons and daughters to endless merrymaking. Every day he holds feasts; there is fun and laughter from morning till night, dancing and singing, and then all sleep soundly in beds adorned with magnificent carving.

"We, too, lived well there. For a whole month Aeolus entertained us, and every evening we had to tell him of the events which took place at Troy, of the Greek heroes, and their fates after the fall of the city. But when I began to ask more and more often whether Aeolus would offer me an escort to continue my voyage, he realised that in spite of all the banquets and kind treatment, I was anxious to leave his court. He did not try to detain me, but personally saw to the preparations for our departure, and finally gave me an unexpected gift for my journey, one such as I could scarcely have expected. He tied up in an oxhide, securely bound with silver cords, all the sea

winds and gales, so that they might not harm us; only gentle Zephyrus was left at liberty. That was the wind we required, who was to lean against our sails all the way to my native island.

"For nine days and nights our sails puffed out before his breath, until on the tenth day the coast of Ithaca came in sight. We could already make out the outlines of the land; the familiar cliffs were in sight, and the crowns of tall trees could be seen sticking out of the thick forests. We could already see the fires beside which the shepherds warmed themselves. For nine days I had not slept, keeping watch at the helm and the sails, and now, tired to death, I was able at last to lie down beside the oxhide, which I had cared for like a dear child, and take a rest. My eyes began to close with exhaustion, and before I knew it I was fast asleep.

"Perhaps I should have staved off my tiredness a little longer, and I daresay I should have told my companions what was in the oxhide I had been given by kind King Aeolus. Then they would not have been so inquisitive, so anxious to open the wind king's gift to see what was inside. But one began to wonder, then another, until, as I slept, the talk went something like this:

" 'Just look at Odysseus! He has fine booty from Troy, while we are returning almost empty-handed. But wherever he goes he knows how to win favour. Now he has received an oxhide from King Aeolus. What can be in it? It will surely not be empty. I daresay it is filled with gold and silver. How nice and plump it is — we ought to take a look and see what it is he doesn't want to share with us!'

"One word led to another, and they egged each other on, until they pounced on the hide, and someone's hand tugged at the silver cord that bound it. The knots gave way; there was a fearful whine, and the bag collapsed, all the winds and gales pouring out of it, rushing round in circles with a howling and swishing, one blowing the ship here, another there; suddenly a storm broke loose, driving us away from Ithaca . . . away from our home — straight back to the island of King Aeolus!

"It was to no avail that my companions bemoaned their deed, it was too late to be sorry. Our ships were mere playthings of the elements when, wretched and exhausted, we reached land again — albeit the shores from where we had set sail ten days earlier.

"And I could only beg the wind king for help once more.

"But this time Aeolus did not receive me kindly at all. When I told him what had happened, he frowned more and more darkly, and when, cautiously and with

humility, I asked him to extend a helping hand, he said to me angrily:

"'Whatever can you be thinking, Odysseus? You received such help from me in returning home as few could expect, and now you are back again! It is not just a question of your tiredness and tardiness, or the envy of your companions. Who knows who sent sleep to your eyes? You have somehow angered the gods, and I will not help anyone who is so ill-favoured with them. Begone with you all!'

"Despondent, cruelly tried and dispirited, we left the island of Aeolus and sailed for the open sea. The ships' keels cut heavily through the waves, and we were obliged to lean on our oars with all our strength.

"We could no longer rely on a following wind and I dared not think what the morrow might bring."

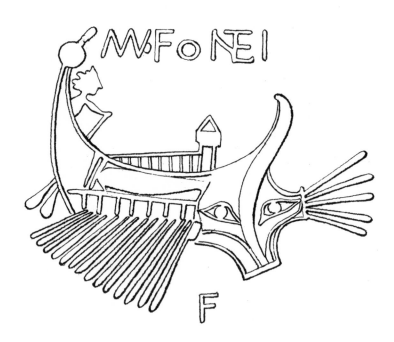

Disaster at the Hands
of the Laestrygones

"Six days and nights passed, and our twelve black ships, with their red-painted prows, roamed back and forth across the sea, seeking a refuge in vain." Everyone listened in awe to Odysseus' story.

"At last, on the seventh day, we sighted land, and to our amazement we were greeted by a perfect harbour. We sailed through straits into a bay enclosed on either side by steep cliffs; its waters were as calm as a forest pool. Eleven ships sailed in and dropped anchor there; only the twelfth, my own, remained on the open sea beside the mouth of the straits. I moored the ship and without

delay climbed up to the top of the cliffs which dropped towards the sea on both sides of the bay. In front of me lay uninhabited lands; only in the distance could I see a line of smoke climbing skywards from somewhere or other. It was essential to find out where we now were but this time I did not want to go scouting myself. Three of our number volunteered to explore our surroundings.

"They had not gone far before they met someone. Beside a spring, close to some city whose outline they could see before them, they came across a young girl who had come

to fetch water. She was extremely tall, a good four or five heads taller than they, but she greeted them kindly. When they asked, she replied willingly that they were on the island of the Laestrygones, ruled by King Antiphates, and that the city they could see was called Telepylus. And she offered at once to take them to the royal seat.

"They accepted her offer gratefully, but when they reached the palace they froze with horror. They were received by a woman twice as tall as the girl they had met: truly she was like a giant statue. She was the queen of the Laestrygones herself. As soon as she saw my men, she began to make a terrible din, and in an instant her husband Antiphates appeared, an ugly monster much bigger even than his wife. He cried out with delight when he saw our poor envoys, running his hands over one of them, and preparing to eat him on the spot. The other two did not wait their turn, but took to their heels and ran back to the ship as fast as they could.

"All at once there was a terrible outcry. The king of the Laestrygones had the alarm sounded, and immediately Laestrygones

came running from all sides, each a huger fellow than the next, and in a little while they had assembled on the cliffs around the calm bay where our fleet was at anchor. Before they could do anything about it, a hail of boulders began to rain down on our friends. The Laestrygones hurled huge pieces of the cliffs, dozens of which fell on our ships, smashing their bows, snapping off masts, splintering their rudders, crashing into their sides and keels, until all eleven, transformed into wrecks, sank beneath the water.

"And the Laestrygones, those fearful ogres, fell upon my poor Greeks, speared them on huge forks, and carried them off like fish, to the sound of their heartrending cries, to feast upon them.

"What could I do for my companions? I was as helpless as they; all I could do was to take my sword and cut the rope which moored my ship, and shout to the sailors not to lose a second. I did not have to tell them twice, for they could see the danger for themselves; they leaned on their oars as never before, the fate of our comrades lending them superhuman strength, and so my ship, the only one left of those that set out from Troy, safely reached the open sea.

"Only now could we breathe more easily — only now could my sailors let go their oars and relax their tired muscles. Saved! We have escaped destruction we wanted to cry, but our tongues were still.

"At that moment we could only think of our companions from the eleven ships we had lost.

"We were unspeakably sad."

Captives of Evil Spells

"And so it was," continued Odysseus, "that I sailed on with a single ship and those of my companions who were left, on into the unknown. The memory of those who had been slain lay heavy upon us still. We were haunted by grim visions of what might be in store for us, and after all the horrors we had experienced our strength began to ebb rapidly away.

"We sailed thus for several days, until our vessel reached the headland of an unknown island. But there were no sudden cries of joy, no one began to dance with excitement. We staggered ashore and fell to the ground as if struck down. Hungry, weak and exhausted, we took two days and nights to recover.

"At dawn on the third day, we were encouraged a little by an unexpected windfall. I ventured away from the coast in the morning mist, and as I was making my way along the forest path to a spring beyond the clearing, a large stag leaped out in front of me. It must have been on its way to water, and I managed to bring it down with a single blow of my spear in its back. It fell, killed instantly, and it was hard work for me to drag it back to my men. It was a fine specimen. Though there were forty-six of us, each received a good portion of roast meat. We ate it with relish until evening; it restored our strength, and made me newly determined.

"I told my companions it was clear that

someone lived in the forest where I had killed the stag, for I had seen smoke rising through the trees. Maybe now we could find out where we were.

"At first they would not hear of it. Uppermost in their minds were the awesome events experienced at the hands of the Laestrygones and the Cyclops. I had to persuade them that by doing nothing we should only seal our own doom. We did not even know if we were on an island or some promontory of the mainland! In the end I proposed that we should cast lots as to who should explore our surroundings. I divided them into two groups of twenty-two men, appointing Eurylochus, our helmsman, as leader of one, while I was to lead the other. Then we placed lots into a helmet, and it was decided: Eurylochus and his group would go scouting. They were not very happy with the idea. They parted from us with tears welling in their eyes, and I have to confess that those of us who remained behind were in much the same state.

"They climbed to the top of a wooded hill, and in a while walked down into a small valley, where a splendid house stood in a well protected spot. It was built of smooth, white stones surrounded by a wall. At the sight of wolves and lions roaming freely around, the men were scared quite out of their wits. But, strange to relate, those wild creatures did not attack them. Quite the opposite. The beasts of prey wagged their tails in a friendly manner and fawned upon them like dogs greeting their returning master when he brings them something good to eat. My scouts took heart, and cautiously approached the gates. Suddenly, they heard sweet, pleasant, delightful singing. It so enticed them that one of them, my good friend Polites, could not resist, and looked over the wall into the house.

"A beautiful young woman with magnificent hair was walking around a loom. She passed the shuttle through the warp, singing that lovely song to herself as she worked.

" 'There is a beautiful woman in there! Let us call out to her — perhaps she will let us in,' Polites called out to the others.

" 'Open up, lady!'

"When she heard them calling, the lovely stranger laid down her shuttle, went to the door, and opened it.

"With a smile she invited my companions inside.

"They could not take their eyes off her, so

much did they like what they saw. They rushed inside, Polites at their head. Only Eurylochus, as if suspecting something, decided he would rather wait outside.

"Meanwhile, the beautiful weaver led my crew into a chamber, offered them seats, and invited them to eat.

"It was strange food she gave them. In it they could make out the taste of honey, cheese, barley flour — all cooked in delicious wine. She also poured some strange juice over this treat. They ate with relish until they were quite full, while the unknown woman looked on with a kind smile.

"Suddenly their heads began to swim strangely. It was as though a sort of veil surrounded them, and out of the mist the beautiful weaver appeared, holding in her hand a twig, with which she struck each of them two light blows. And at that instant hairs grew from their skin, their heads lengthened into snouts, and there was the sound of desperate snorting. In a few moments twenty-two pigs were running about the room.

"She drove them out, ignoring their mournful grunts, and goaded them into a sty behind the house. There she threw them some beech-nuts and acorns to eat, and closed the sty door.

"Breathless and terror-stricken, his eyes nearly popping out of his head, Eurylochus came running up to tell us of the terrible fate that had befallen his men.

" 'We must go to them at once,' I decided, when my helmsman, whom we could scarcely get a sensible word out of, had finally stammered out what had happened. 'Show us the way!'

" 'Go back there?' cried Eurylochus in alarm. 'Are you out of your mind, Odysseus? No one can help that lot any more — it would be better to be on our way as soon as possible! Who knows what might befall us!'

" 'He's right! Let's go, let's get out of here,' the rest piped up, and if I was not to leave my poor men to their fate, there was nothing for it but to set off on my own.

"I do not know how I should have fared if the god Hermes himself had not come to my aid.

"He appeared in front of me as I was nearing the white stone house, though I had not the slightest idea how to deliver my friends from the power of that evil spell. He looked like a young man with the first fluff on his chin, and by way of greeting he pressed his hand sympathetically into mine.

" 'Where are you off to in such a hurry, unhappy man?' he asked. 'I know you want to save your companions, but do you know in whose power they are? That enchantress, the goddess Circe! She will listen to neither tears nor prayers, but will turn you, too, into a pig! You'll join them in the sty!'

" 'Then am I to leave them to their fate?' I asked, my heart heavy with sorrow.

" 'No! You will save them, but you must do as I tell you.'

"He gave me a special sort of herb, with a black root and a flower as white as milk.

" 'I will give you this precious herb, which only the gods and those who belong to their family can find and pick. It is a magic plant, and will protect you from destruction. When you meet Circe, she will offer you food, and will put a magic juice on it. But first you must eat this root, which will destroy the power of her dreadful potion. You may eat

and drink what she gives you; when she strikes you with her magic twig to turn you into a pig, you will draw your sword and leap upon her. She will flatter you, tell you she likes you, tempt you. But take no notice. She must swear an oath that she will harm neither you nor your companions. Then you will be in no danger from her, and she will do anything you wish.'

"I thanked Hermes and, with a pounding heart, I was soon knocking at the door of Circe's white house. When she heard me, she opened up and I found myself looking into an exquisitely beautiful face framed with long locks of hair.

"She smiled at me as if she were waiting for me, and motioned for me to enter. Inside, she offered me a seat decorated in silver, and poured me a full cup of wine. She dropped her magic potion in it in such a way that I could not see, and then watched with satisfaction as I emptied the cup drop by drop.

"When I had finished, her kind smile began to harden, and her sweet face grew sterner. Then she reached out behind her; suddenly she was holding a twig, and Circe struck me several times.

" 'Into the sty with you!' she cried. 'You have drunk the magic potion! You are a pig, and you belong with the rest of them!'

" 'I have drunk a magic potion?'

"I leapt up out of the chair, drew my sword, and hurled myself upon her as if to stab her there and then.

" 'Then you are mistaken — your magic spells are of no use against me! You will not make a pig out of *me*!'

"She looked astonished; then she sank to the ground and firmly hugged my knees.

" 'How is it that my wine had no effect on you?' she began to sob, suddenly confused. 'It has always worked before: three or four sips were enough, and I changed them all into pigs. And you drank a whole cup, and nothing happened! Nothing! This can mean only one thing — that you are Odysseus, the son of the Ithacan king, Laertes! For it was foretold to me by Hermes, messenger of Zeus, that he would come to me on his way home from Troy. But why are you holding your sword like that? Why is it pointing at my breast? I welcome you in my house; let us be friends. Come, I will have a banquet prepared in your honour! Stay here with me!'

" 'No, no, no, Circe,' I said, shaking my head, and still holding the point of my sword at her. 'While my friends are locked in your sty in the form of pigs, there will be no friendship between us.'

" 'I will have a banquet prepared,' she repeated, stubbornly, 'and tell the servants to make ready a bath for you, and to bring you fine robes and a cloak. We will spend a fine evening together. I like you, Odysseus. And if you must hear it, I swear that no danger threatens you or your companions.'

"But still I insisted.

" 'I will not eat a morsel, Circe, or touch a cup, until I see my companions back in their human form. You have sworn to do it — so release them from your spell!'

"She sighed, then stood up without a word, took her magic twig, and left the room. I followed her.

"At the fence around the pigsty we stopped. She drew back the bolt and twenty-two pigs rushed out, snorting. Circe touched them lightly with her wand and

rubbed each of them with some sort of ointment. The hairs fell from their bodies, their snouts changed back into human faces, and their snorting became human voices again. All of a sudden there in front of me stood my companions, including Polites, and they were even younger and stronger than before.

"They surrounded me, embraced me, took my hands, and even began to weep with joy.

" 'I have kept my oath,' said Circe. 'And now, Odysseus, bring along the rest of your company who stayed on the ship. Let them beach the ship and leave their belongings with me, that they may rest. From now on you are my guests!'

"Only then did I accept her invitation, and the others were glad to join me. Eurylochus alone refused to trust the sudden kindness of this goddess of enchantment.

" 'Beware lest Odysseus himself is trapped, and you with him,' he muttered to the men. 'It was he who took us into the Cyclops' cave, and several of us paid with their lives. Can you trust that enchantress not to try again?'

"But in the end he, too, allowed himself

to be persuaded, and the whole crew went to stay in Circe's house.

"We had no idea how pleasant our stay there would be! Her companions, beautiful wood and water nymphs, saw to it that we had enough good food and drink, and looked after our entertainment in every way.

"Month after month went by in merriment and pastimes, and before we knew it a whole year had passed.

"But though we had a fine time, my men began to feel homesick. Day after day someone would come to me and remind me that although we were enjoying ourselves, we should launch our ship again, raise the mast and set sail.

"So, one day, we told Circe that the time had come for us to go, the hour of parting was at hand. Strangely enough, she took the news calmly, and when, in the evening, I told her of my decision, she was even kinder than usual to me.

" 'I will not keep you here, Odysseus,' she told me, as she led me for the last time from the richly laden table to her bed. 'But I must tell you one thing: if you want your voyage to continue auspiciously, you must learn of all the things that may await you on the journey back to Ithaca. You must know the intentions of the gods.'

" 'And how might I do that, Circe?' I asked with a smile. 'No one in the whole world can tell me!'

" 'No one in the world — you are right,' she replied. 'You will have to go elsewhere.'

" 'I do not understand, Circe.'

" 'You must, dear Odysseus, go down into

the underworld! There, in the kingdom of Hades and fearful Persephone, you will find the ghost of the blind seer, Tiresias, long-since dead. He can tell you your fate.'

"At these words my blood froze. My head began to spin, and I fell backwards in a kind of faint, clutching my hands to my temples, in which the blood had suddenly begun to pulse. Indeed I wanted nothing more than to cease to exist, never more to see the light of day.

" 'What — may a mortal venture to undertake such a journey?' I managed to ask. 'Descend into the kingdom of Hades, where the souls of the dead dwell? Down into the underworld? Goddess, I do not even know how to get there!'

" 'Do not worry about that, dear King of Ithaca! You shall raise your mast, hoist your sail, and the god of all the winds and I will see to the rest. Your ship will reach the great river Oceanus, beyond which is the grove of the goddess Persephone and the entrance to the underworld. You will easily recognise the place by the slender black poplars and the weeping willows which grow there. When you land, you will set off on' your own. Then you will see a cliff at the point where two foaming rivers meet — there you must dig a hole and beside it sacrifice to the

memory of the dead a black sheep and a black ram. The scent of their blood will attract the ghosts of the dead, but you must not allow any of them to drink the blood of the sacrificial animals until you have asked Tiresias what fate awaits you.'

"How heavy was my heart the next morning when I told my companios what more we must endure before our ship was again directed towards our native Ithaca!

"It was just as I had expected. They began to sob with grief, and some almost tore their hair with despair. Like small children they began to beg me and implore me to postpone our departure. And when I told them we had no choice, they began to drown their fears in wine. One of them, the youngest of the crew, Elpenor, paid dearly for it. He was so drunk on the day of our departure that he fell from the terrace of Circe's house and broke his neck.

"For our parting Circe dressed in a beautiful white gown of the finest material and wore a magnificent belt embroidered with gold. She hid her face behind a veil. She was quite radiant, her long locks of hair cascading down over her shoulders, and it was difficult to take our leave of her after a year of such pleasure. She escorted us to our ship, and with her own hands tied to the prow the black ram and sheep which were to be sacrificed in the underworld. Then she left without a word. We were all close to tears, and she appeared similarly moved . . .

"We launched the ship, and the oarsmen fastened their oars in position and made ready. Hardly had the keel cut the surface, when the sail filled, the yard creaked, and the sheets drew taut. A strong wind drove our ship forward.

"The enchantress Circe had fulfilled her promise.

"Our black vessel with its red prow slipped through the waves like a bird through the air, towards the gloomy corners of the earth where the spirits of the underworld are ruled over by the mighty Hades and his wife Persephone."

The Prophesy of Tiresias

"The way to the underworld is grim and inhospitable. All is veiled in unrelenting mist and thick cloud. The sun never shines, and no star twinkles in the sky. Only a heavy darkness shrouds the place where the great river Oceanus flows, in which all the waters of the earth, all the rivers and seas, have their beginning. It is from here that the sun, the moon and the stars rise, and it is to this place that they return, after their journey across the heavenly dome." Odysseus' terrible tale went on.

"We sailed to this grim corner of the earth, to the banks with their weeping willows and black poplars, safely driven on by a favourable wind, as Circe had foretold.

"I stepped on to the shore, dug a pit and prepared the sacrifice. First there was milk and honey, then wine, and then water and barley flour. Then I slaughtered the black ram and sheep. Their dark blood filled the pit, and as I called upon the souls of all the dead to come forth, the murky, blurred outlines of figures began to appear from the grey mists.

"There were many of them, and they approached from all sides, some groaning, others muttering unintelligibly. They

surrounded me, and suddenly I recognised a number of familiar faces, among the first of them Elpenor, our youngest crew-member not long dead. He called out to me plaintively to remember to offer a sacrifice for him when I got home, and to see to it that he had a dignified funeral.

"The spirits came closer, pressing towards the pit which held the blood of the sacrificial victims, and even my mother appeared among them. But I could allow no one, not even her, to drink the sacrificial blood. I drove them back, sword in hand, recalling what Circe had told me, and looked around desperately for Tiresias. At last one of the figures spoke to me, and I knew from his golden sceptre that it was Tiresias himself.

" 'Put away your sword,' he told me, and when I stepped aside he bent over the pit, drank some of the blood, and then motioned to me and spoke to me again.

" 'I think I know, Odysseus, why you have come to this mournful place to see me. You will be none too pleased with what I have to tell you, son of Laertes. There are difficult days ahead of you. Poseidon is most angry with you for blinding his son, the Cyclops Polyphemus. But in spite of his anger, you — and your companions — may reach home safely, if you follow my counsel.

● THE PROPHESY OF TIRESIAS ●

Listen! Your journey back will take you to the island of Thrinacie. There you will find at pasture a herd of cows and sheep belonging to the sun god Helios. None of you must touch them, or your ship, your companions, and you yourself will be threatened with destruction. And even if you escape all dangers, you will return home only after long wanderings, quite alone, without your companions, in a foreign ship, like a beggar. And at home you will find all brought to nothing — the kingdom ravaged, your house in ruins, your wife surrounded by dozens of suitors. You will not avoid a fierce struggle with those arrogant pretenders to your throne. It will be a cruel and bloody contest, and you will be obliged to use your cunning. When it is over, do not forget to make peace with Poseidon by means of a sacrifice. Offer him a ram, a bull and a boar, Odysseus! I will give you a sign when the moment has come. Only then can you look forward to long years of peace and contentment for you and your people.'

"Tiresias' spirit began to fade, as if he wished to depart from me. I held out a hand to him to keep him there.

" 'Is that all you will tell me, Tiresias? Tell me one thing, at least — I have seen many familiar faces here. My mother, the Greek nobles, my comrades in arms from Troy. I should like to speak to them at least — tell me how I am to do it!'

"The vanishing spirit replied as if from a great distance: 'All you allow to drink the blood of your sacrifice will speak to you, and will tell you the truth about all you ask.'

"My mind was made up. My mother was standing near, and she fixed me with a pleading gaze. I hurried over to her and motioned to her. Her lips had scarcely touched the sacrificial blood, when I heard her sobbing voice.

" 'My son, my child, how did you come to this sad place? Are you only now returning from the walls of Troy? Have you not been in Ithaca yet?'

" 'I come, dear mother, to hear the prophesy of Tiresias. But tell me, what is happening at home? Do they not think me dead? Is Penelope bringing up my dear Telemachus? Or has she married some rich nobleman? Does anyone remember me there?'

" 'Penelope is faithful to you,' my mother's ghost whispered warmly. 'She has many suitors, but she still believes you will return. Telemachus, too, is alive and well, and your father, too, though he has moved from the palace to the country and lives there with his servants. He tills the soil, looks after the orchards and vines, and is troubled by one longing only — to see you once more! Ah, how well I know it! Is that not why I became so weak, and suffered so long that in the end I left the world of the living? I was not destroyed by sudden sickness or unhappy accident, but by a measureless, unfulfilled longing to see you!'

"Tears came to my eyes. I wanted to press my mother to my breast, but the faint shadow which spoke to me in that sweet familiar voice was getting further and further away from me. It was as if I were embracing thin air.

" 'Mother,' I whispered, 'why do you not let me embrace you?'

"But I heard only her weakening, heartfelt whisper: 'Thus it is, dear son, when the licking flames eat the flesh and bones of

man. Only a flickering shadow remains. That is the fate of us all. But go back where you belong, among the living, and remember what I have told you, so that you may tell your faithful Penelope, too.'

"My mother's ghost vanished, dissolving like a cloud, and other figures drew near.

"And how many of them there were who came to drink the blood of my sacrifice!

"Agamemnon, the renowned king of Mycenae, greeted me along with his entire company, and warned me to beware when I landed on Ithacan soil; for someone might well plot to assassinate me, as his treacherous cousin Aegisthus had murdered him.

"Patroclus appeared, who fought so bravely with the Trojans in the armour of Achilles, until he was cut down by Hector.

"The fearless warrior Antilochus, son of the old King Nestor of Pylos, greeted me with a glance, and then Achilles himself, boldest of all the Greeks, the pride of their army, appeared.

"Achilles, too, wet his lips with sacrificial blood; he was most noble, dignified, worthy of honour — just as I had known him when we stood together at arms beneath the

standards of Agamemnon and Menelaus.

"'Achilles, son of Peleus, my old comrade,' I addressed him, trembling, 'I see that even here in the underworld you are as honoured as you were in your life on earth.'

" 'Surely you will not praise the kingdom of Hades? It were better to be a servant in the lowliest farmstead in the world of the living than to be king here!' he replied bitterly, and began to ask me about his people, his father, and above all his son — had he proved himself in battle?

"How his face glowed with pleasure when I told him the lad had always been in the thick of the fray, bold but at the same time prudent, in short, a son any Greek would be proud of! As he departed from me at his usual swift pace, seeming to slide across the underworld meadow, Achilles glanced back several times and looked at me, an expression of blissful contentment on his face.

"I also met Ajax, son of the king of Salamis. I once quarrelled with him over which of us should have Achilles' rare armour; I had long ago ceased to derive any joy from the fact that I had gained it, and now I should have liked to make amends to him. But he passed me without a word, though I invited him to forget our differences.

"And other spirits came near me. I saw famed women, Alcmene, mother of Heracles, and beautiful Ariadne, daughter of the Cretan king, Minos, the Theban queen Epicasta, mother of Oedipus, and many others. I also saw Agamemnon's great-grandfather, Tantalus, punished for his godlessness with eternal hunger and thirst. He stood in a pool of water, which splashed against his chin, but if he bent down to take a drink the water receded, soaking into the ground. If he wanted to satisfy his hunger, and reached out for one of the apples or pears which grew above his head, a wind came and blew the branches out of reach.

"I saw, too, the dreadful fate of Sisyphus. Ceaselessly, and with all his strength, he rolled a huge boulder up a steep hill, and it always rolled back down again just as he got to the top. Again and again Sisyphus began anew his endless, ungrateful task.

"New figures drew near, gathering around me; many of them moaned and groaned; there was an ever louder shouting and whining, until I was suddenly seized with terror lest I should never get out of this realm of despair. What if Persephone should send the fearful Gorgon's head with its hair of poisonous snakes? A single glance at it would be enough to turn me to stone. I had to get away, away from this grim kingdom of the dead!

"I grasped the hilt of my sword firmly and ran back to our ship."

The Song of the Sirens

" 'Friends, I heard with my own ears the renowned Tiresias, and his prophesy says we may come safely home. If we act as we should, we shall finally land on Ithacan shores, though it will not be easy. So let us put all our strength into it! Forward!'

"These were my first words on reaching the ship and seeing my companions again," Odysseus continued.

"I did not need to encourage them to leave this grim shore of weeping willows and black poplars. And all were greatly relieved to see me alive and well. The oarsmen hurried to their places; the rope was untied, and the ship set off downstream along Oceanus, carried along by the oars and a gentle breeze, back to the wide blue sea.

"We stopped off just for a while on the island of the enchantress Circe, to give Elpenor a fitting funeral, as I had promised him in the underworld, and after a day's rest we set off once more.

"The ship ploughed through the foam-decked sea; a following wind gave her good speed, and my men put all their effort into their rowing. All felt our prospects were

good, for had not Tiresias' prophesy been an auspicious one? I alone felt that all was not yet over by any means. That evening, before we left, Circe had revealed to me beneath a shroud of the utmost secrecy that before we reached the island of Thrinacie, where the herds of the sun god Helios grazed, two great dangers awaited us. One was the island of the Sirens, those half-human, half-bird creatures who allure unwitting sailors with their delightful song, and suck the blood from the bodies of those foolish enough to land. The other was the straits where on one side is the cave of the twelve-legged monster with six dog's heads, Scylla, and on the other the underwater monster Charybdis, who six times daily creates a deadly whirlpool which swallows ships up. Each was more dangerous than other, and no ship had yet managed to sail safely between the two of them. I trembled with horror when Circe told me of this, and engraved her advice on my

memory. How fortunate it was I followed it! How lucky I told my companions of it in time, and made them follow it too!

"We learned that we were near the island of the Sirens when we were suddenly becalmed. The wind dropped as suddenly as if a magic wand had been waved. Hardly a wave stirred the surface. The ship stood still, its sail hanging limply. The crew rolled up the canvas, stowed it, and sat down at the oars again. The ship moved off. That was the moment I had to make my move.

"'Friends,' I said, 'can you see that island on the horizon? Perhaps you can make out the meadows filled with flowers. Perhaps you even think you hear a faint singing. Do you? Well listen to what I have to say: on that island live two Sirens, creatures with a woman's head and a bird's body. They can sing more sweetly than anyone on Earth, but woe betide him who allows himself to be allured by their song and steps ashore! He

has thrown his life away! When we get nearer, you will see piles of human bones — their victims. Only one thing can save you — you must stuff your ears with beeswax, so that you may not fall victim to the enchantment of their song. And you must tie me up and bind me to the mast, so that I cannot move. As we sail past, whatever happens you must not release me, even if I should beg you or order you to do so!'

"It was extremely difficult to make our preparations before the ship got within hailing distance of the island. My men, their ears stopped up with wax, pulled hard at the oars, and our ship glided across the water as they rowed. Only I, tied hand and foot to the mast, could hear the enchanting, enthralling, delightful song of the Sirens.

" 'Odysseus, pride of the Achaeans, clever and renowned warrior, why do you pass us by with your black-painted ship?' they sang. 'Why do you not come and let us delight you with our song, as others do when they pass by? Step ashore and listen to it! Or will your companions not allow you to? Then jump overboard and swim to our island; you will have a wonderful time here!'

"The longer I listened, the more I liked their song. Everything within me sang with them; I had an inexpressible desire to listen to their delightful voices there on the island. I was drawn towards it by the enchanting song, and began to beg my fellows: 'Untie me! Leave me here! I must go to the island of the Sirens; I want to hear their sweet song. I order you, untie me!'

"I ordered, begged, threshed about so violently that the mast shook, and it seemed I might soon break free of my bonds. Finally Eurylochus and Perimedes jumped up and tied me down again.

"And the song still tempted me, and I kept turning my face to the island, even though our ship was leaving it behind now, and the voices of the Sirens were growing fainter and fainter.

"Only when we were too far away to hear the treacherous song at all could my companions take the beeswax from their ears and untie me from the mast . . ."

A Pair of Sea Monsters

"We were able to relax only for a short while." Odysseus shuddered at the memory.

"We had scarcely escaped the clutches of the Sirens, when a huge column of water arose in front of us, reaching up to the sky.

"Even from a considerable distance we could hear the fearful noise it made, so loud that our ship shook from stem to stern. The sea was churned up so fiercely that the oars leapt from the rowers' hands.

"It was a dreadful place; only one ship, the huge *Argo*, with fifty oars, in which King Jason had once set out to seek the golden fleece, had ever passed through without difficulty, but only because Zeus' own wife, Hera, had taken it under her protection!

"Then two steep cliffs emerged in front of us. They soared up towards the sky, and we could not even see to the top of them; their peaks were concealed in thick, ominous clouds. In a cave in one of the cliffs lived the first of the monsters Circe had warned me about, the grotesque Scylla.

"This horrible creature has twelve legs, six heads, and three rows of teeth in each set of jaws. She hunts dolphins, seals and all creatures which live in the sea. But woe betide any ship which sails nearby. The monster hurls herself upon it and tears one sailor after another from it with her fearful claws until her hunger is satisfied.

"But Charybdis is more terrible still. She lives close by Scylla, beside the smaller cliff, on which a tall fig tree grows. Six times daily she sets the waters spinning in a fearful whirlpool. Pity the unsuspecting sailors whose boat is passing at that time! Charybdis draws them in like a piece of driftwood, and buries them in the deep for ever.

"I saw my companions stiffen with fear as we approached the spot. The oars fell from their hands, a cold sweat broke out on their temples, and their faces paled with terror.

" 'Friends, let us not give up! We have survived so many dangers; nothing worse than we suffered at the hands of the Cyclops can await us now,' I cried out in order to encourage them. 'Take up your oars again and stay close to the larger of the cliffs! Charybdis would swallow us all, but I daresay we shall manage to escape Scylla. Let us sail on, and you, helmsman, do not forget: stay close to the larger of the cliffs! If Scylla should appear, I will fight her!'

"It was Circe who had advised me to try to get past Scylla, but not to provoke her if we could help it. Still, I put on my helmet, picked up my shield, and with my spears at the ready, prepared to meet the monster. But nothing happened — it seemed as

though Scylla had stayed in her lair and was going to leave us alone.

"We sailed into the straits, the tension mounting in us all. Close to the smaller of the cliffs the surface of the water grew rough, with a terrible screeching and rumbling, as if the sea were boiling violently, and a huge column of water splashed up to the very tops of the cliffs.

"Then, with a wild roar, a violent whirlpool began to spin round and round, the cliff shook, and the water fell back with the speed of lightning, until the sandy bottom was revealed.

"While we stared breathlessly at the raging Charybdis, shivering with fear lest we should be drawn into it, an ominous barking came from the other side, from the taller of the cliffs. Scylla was howling in her cave!

"Suddenly, from that direction, six long necks were thrust out like huge tentacles — on the end of them heads with three rows of teeth which snapped at our vessel. And then I saw only the arms and legs of those who disappeared into Scylla's hideous throats. They yelled, screamed, squirmed like worms which an angler has stuck on his hook — but there was nothing I could do to help.

What use to me were spears and a sword? What harm could they do to a monster like that? I stood like a statue and my blood ran cold. That image has remained with me ever since.

"Thanks to the efforts of the oarsmen we had now moved away from both cliffs; we were approaching the grassy shores of the island of Thrinacie, and I could still see my helpless crewmen stretching out their arms and calling my name for the last time.

"It was only when I heard the lowing of cows and the bleating of sheep from a pen somewhere on land that I came to my senses. I recalled the warning words of Tiresias, and realised at once we must not land on this island! Our ship must avoid these shores at all costs!"

The Herds of Helios

"For the first time on our voyage," explained Odysseus, "it was I who was against going ashore.

"Thrinacie appeared in front of the red-painted prow of our black ship as a slender strip of green on the horizon, and I could well imagine how attractive the idea of a few days' rest was to my sailors. I summoned them and, taxing my eloquence to the utmost, warned them once again. It seemed to me that I could not have spoken more convincingly. They would surely understand: it was better to continue, not to drop anchor, not to set foot on this corner of the Earth.

"But when I had finished, I saw in the eyes of my companions weariness, lack of understanding, and perhaps even suspicion. It was Eurylochus, and not I, who gave voice to the general feeling, when without inhibition he said:

" 'And why should we not have at least a few hours' rest? Are we made of iron, as you seem to be, Odysseus? We have not slept properly, and after our toil at the oars none of us can feel a bone in his body — and suddenly you do not even want us to stretch out peacefully on dry land! Not only that, but night is upon us, and who is to say whether or not there will be a storm? Then we might lose our ship! I propose we should land! We shall eat our fill in comfort and sleep through the night, and in the morning we can raise anchor again and sail on.'

"He had scarcely finished speaking when there was a murmur of agreement.

" 'Eurylochus·is right,' came voices from all sides. 'Let us do as he suggests!'

"I realised that it was no use trying to persuade them.

" 'Then you are against my proposal?' I cried. 'Very well — you shall have your way! But in that case you must all swear on the spot that none of you will touch a scrap of food other than what we have with us. If any beast should appear, such as a nice sheep or ram or a fat cow, no one shall so much as notice it; no one shall lay a finger on it!'

" 'Not a finger! We solemnly swear by Zeus himself!' Eurylochus promised readily, and the others repeated the solemn oath after him.

"The ship drew close to the shore, and then sailed into a narrow bay enclosed on all sides. It beached at a spot where fresh water flowed into the sea.

"We went ashore, brought food from the ship, and prepared supper. The wine with which we washed down that tasty meal

revived memories and loosened tongues. It seemed to us as if all those who had left us forever during the last few days of our voyage were still there with us. We heard again the angry screech of the waves stirred up by the greedy Charybdis and the ominous howling and barking of the six-headed Scylla.

"Weariness was overtaking us, and we were seized with a longing to see again the comrades who had been wrenched from us; then, at last, sleep overcame us one by one.

"But we did not sleep long. After midnight, as morning began to approach, we were awoken by a gale and a terrible storm. The sky above the sea and the land was covered by dark clouds; lightning flashes came thick and fast, illuminating the skies, and we only just managed to drag the ship to a safer haven, into a rocky cove at the end of

the bay. We supposed we would wait until the storm blew itself out, that the raging elements would calm down again, and that we should be able to continue on our way.

"But the wind did not drop. Not even by morning, nor by the next evening. There was no question of setting sail. The enormous waves would have smashed our ship to pieces before it reached the open sea.

"I summoned the crew for a council.

"'Friends, we have enough food and drink on board ship, and sooner or later this bad weather must cease. Until then our supplies will hold out,' I encouraged my companions. 'The important thing is that no one should think of helping himself to fresh beef or mutton! You know that all the animals on this island belong to the sun god, Helios, and he hears and sees everything in the world.'

"They heard what I had to say, nodded their heads, and surely wondered why I kept repeating my warning, since we had plenty of wine and meat on board our ship.

"But the storm went on and on. Night followed day, and day night, and the sea was as rough as ever. Before the month was out our supplies had run short, and then one day we had nothing to eat.

"We started to hunt, out of necessity. Now and again we managed to shoot a bird, and once in a while had a fish dangling at the end of our lines, but these humble provisions were not nearly enough for so many men, and hunger ate at their insides. They had cramp in their stomachs, a gnawing pain in their guts, and a dry feeling in their mouths.

"I decided to go off on my own and beg the gods for help; perhaps Pallas Athene or one of the others would be able to find a way for us to get off this island. I set off by myself along the beach and then went inland, where, in a quiet spot which seemed like a sacrificial grove, I called out with all my heart to the gods high on Olympus. Then, either out of weariness or through their will, in the middle of my prayers I fell into a treacherous sleep.

"Meanwhile, hunger had taken the last remnants of caution away from my companions. Scarcely had I left, when Eurylochus himself took advantage of my absence and began to egg them on:

"'Are we to die here of hunger, my friends, when fat sheep and cows graze in

meadows only a few paces away? We have heard that these herds belong to Helios, and that he would be angry with us if we were to touch them. But let us do it like this: we will pick a couple of nice animals and offer them to the gods as a sacrifice to make amends, and there will still be enough to stem our hunger. And we will also vow to build a splendid temple to Helios when we get back to Ithaca. To die is a terrible thing, but to die of hunger is the worst death of all! So why should Helios be angry with us if we kill a few of his sheep to fill our stomachs? All we want is to stay alive — no more! And if he were to be angry with us, and with the help of the other gods maybe broke our ship on the seas, I'll tell you straight — I should rather be washed away at once by a wave in

a storm than to leave the world slowly in a painful death from hunger!'

"Alas, the others needed no persuasion. The minds of my companions at that moment were occupied with one desire only: to eat their fill and to satisfy their hunger.

"They gathered the last of their strength and hurried to a nearby meadow, where a herd of Helios' cows was grazing. They surrounded them, prayed fervently to the gods, and then one after another slaughtered those sacred cows with their broad foreheads and curved horns.

"My men stripped the hides, cut out the best pieces of meat from the rump, which they then placed in a double layer of lard; since there was no wine left with which to

sprinkle this offering, as was the custom, they had to use water. First they roast the meat from the rump which was offered to the gods, then they ate the heart, liver and kidneys, and finally stuck the remainder of the meat on the spit.

"The smoke rose up from their fire. Delicious aromas wafted far and wide. I smelt them even in my deep sleep.

"Suddenly I was awake, and knew at once what was happening. 'Zeus, ruler of Olympus, and all you other gods of the sacred mountain — why did you let me sleep?' I wailed aloud. 'Or did you put me to sleep deliberately, because you knew that my companions were preparing to commit this terrible, sacrilegious deed? If only Helios might relent and be merciful to us!'

"But I felt my plea was in vain. It was as if I knew that Helios was already turning to the gods of Olympus and asking for the sternest of punishments for those who had killed and eaten cows from his sacred herd, of which he was so proud, and which he looked forward to seeing at the end of each day's journey across the heavenly orb. He was most offended, and Calypso, the divine nymph, later revealed to me how he threatened Zeus himself: that he would never again sit in his heavenly chariot in order to pour sunshine on the world of the mortals over which Zeus rules, but would go for ever to the underworld, to the realm of grim Hades. It was only with difficulty that Zeus calmed him, swearing to avenge this insult and punish its perpetrators with a single bolt of thunder.

"I scarcely caught my breath before rushing back to my crew. From afar I called to them, shouted and railed at them,

remonstrated with them, wept; I accused Eurylochus, then the others, one by one, but it was no use now; the cows from the sacred herd had been killed.

"And it seemed that the gods were already showing their ill will, their wrath at this insolent deed. The skins taken from the cows began to move uncannily in the morning light; the roasting oxen lowed pitifully as they turned on the spits. Truly their fate had now been decided, but hunger had taken over. For a full six days my companions feasted, deaf to my reproaches, indifferent to my warning words, not even noticing that I refused to touch a mouthful.

"At dawn on the seventh day the gale dropped and the sea suddenly grew calm enough for us to venture out of the bay. We quickly raised the mast and hoisted our white sails, and before long Thrinacie was lost from view.

"There was a clear blue sky above us and as far as the eye could see the surface of the water was calm. Small waves lapped against the sides of our ship, the sun playing with them in carefree mood, and it seemed to the sailors that this pleasant hour would never cease.

"It was this very moment that mighty Zeus, ruler of the clouds and storms, had chosen to seal our fate. All of a sudden a heavy, metallic cloud spread over our heads. The winds howled, striking our ship a mighty blow and breaking the forestays. The mast groaned, snapped like a splinter, and fell back into the ship, taking with it the rest of the rigging. There was a dull thud as it struck the helmsman square on the head. The terrible blow knocked him unconscious and hurled him overboard.

"Immediately there was a terrible roar of thunder and we were all dazzled by a blinding flash of lightning, hurled at our ship by an enraged Zeus! The whole ship shuddered, and a thick, sickening smell of sulphur filled the air. I fell to my knees, stunned, and when, a few moments later, I came to my senses, I saw that the thunderbolt had flung all my companions into the sea.

"For a second I saw them wrestle with huge walls of waves, which dragged them mercilessly down into the depths, and before long they had all vanished from sight. I was left alone on the ship.

"I did not know what to do, and ran back and forth like one possessed. The ship was a wreck; the mighty waves had caved in her hull, the mast was crashing back and forth. In the end I lashed it with the strong mainstay, plaited from bull's hide, to the remains of the ship's skeleton.

"Then I climbed onto that raft, those few pieces of timber, and clung to it for dear life. I do not know how long the storm used me as its plaything. I only know that as the ferocity of one wind seemed to abate, another began to blow the same frantic way, driving me this way and that all night. When the sun rose I saw nearby a familiar pair of cliffs — the rocky homes of Scylla and Charybdis. It was not long before Charybdis set her whirlpool of doom in motion. In a few more moments it would have swallowed me up along with my raft, the remains of the keel and the mast. With a huge effort I raised myself up to the cliff, catching hold of the sturdy fig tree's branches; I was left hanging there like a bat.

"In the meantime Charybdis engulfed my raft, and I waited anxiously to see whether she would disgorge it again. After a long time the waters turned once more, spitting out onto the surface a few splintered slithers of wood — remnants of smashed ribs, tiny pieces of the keel and the mast were all that remained of my once-proud ship. But this flotsam was my only hope!

"I let go of the fig tree, falling into the water beside these scraps of wood, and struggled back to the surface; then I tried to use my arms as oars in order to keep my balance and direction as well as possible. Perhaps Zeus took pity on me, and certainly Pallas Athene was on my side, or how else could I have passed by the cave of Scylla unscathed and escaped to the open sea?

"Then the current carried me along, more dead than alive, for a whole nine days.

"On the tenth night, when I was no longer aware of what was happening, I was thrown ashore by the waves on the island of Calypso, the divine nymph.

"I was saved, yet I was a captive. I was on Ogygia, whence after many years the will of the gods has brought me here to you."

The Departure

Odysseus finished his account, and for a long time the listeners in the banqueting hall sat silent and spellbound. The eyes of the noblemen of Phaeacia still hung upon his lips. Queen Arete, lost in thought, stroked the splendid drape of her throne. Nausicaa breathed a sigh of relief. King Alcinous raised his head.

"You have suffered much, Odysseus," he said. "But now your troubles are over once and for all. We will take you home — have no fear. Nor shall you leave us empty-handed; I have already had the chest filled with fine clothes loaded on the ship, along with the golden cup I gave you and the gifts of our noble captains; now I give you still more gifts that you may remember us well. You never know when you might need them."

Odysseus raised his cup for a last toast.

"Mighty and renowned King Alcinous, and you, noblemen of Phaeacia, how can I express my infinite gratitude? With your help I shall be able to fulfil a wish I have nurtured for many years . . . May the gods of Olympus show you favour for ever! May you live with your wives and children on your hospitable island in never-ending joy!"

"And you, noble queen," he said, turning to Arete, "may you be happy to the end of your days, and may each of them bring you new joy! And may you take pleasure in your children, in the love of your husband, and the honour of all Phaeacians!"

All drank a silent toast, moved by Odysseus' gratitude and his narrative, and Alcinous said:

"Tomorrow at this time you will be on the open sea, far from us . . . I think it is time we retired. You have a journey before you, and you must rest. You, and all those who will sail with you."

And the guests began to rise from their seats. One after another they left, each bowing to Odysseus and taking his leave of him, until he was left alone with the members of the royal family.

"I wish you good night," said Odysseus, "and once again thank you for everything, king and queen."

Stepping slowly, half out of tiredness and half out of hesitation, he walked across the banqueting hall to go to his chamber, where

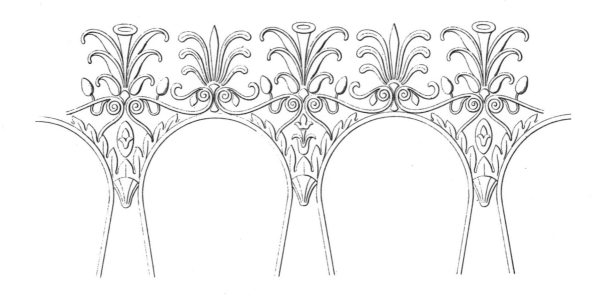

the servants had already laid the beautiful red covers on his carved bed.

At the door he stopped.

Nausicaa was standing there, eyes cast down, hands hanging loosely by her side, like the motionless statue of some goddess.

He lightly touched her shoulder and quietly, in a whisper, said:

"A pity I cannot stay, Nausicaa!"

Then he strode resolutely out of the banqueting hall.

He wished with all his heart for morning to come. To hear the rush of the water. To see the wind fill the sail. To feel the spray thrown up by the swift ship's prow as it sliced through the waves. To cry out with joy when he became the first to sight on the horizon the line of that dear, familiar land whence his endless, wearisome and blighted travels were leading him.

Sleep? Rest? There was no hope of that!

All night long he tossed and turned on the beautiful red bedspread; but he did not sleep a wink. He could not wait for morning.

But in the dawn, when he stepped aboard the ship, he was dizzy with tiredness, and was glad when the farewells were over. He was pleased to find they had prepared for him in the stern a comfortable corner with carpets and bedspreads to lie on. Excited, anxious, shaking, impatient, he crawled into them and fell asleep at last, peacefully content for the first time in nineteen years.

It was a deep, deep sleep, and the ship glided along like a swift and nimble swallow. When dawn broke again in the east, they were drawing near to Ithaca, to the bay of the sea god Phorcys.

They sailed in safely, for the Phaeacians knew it of old. They made for land at the far

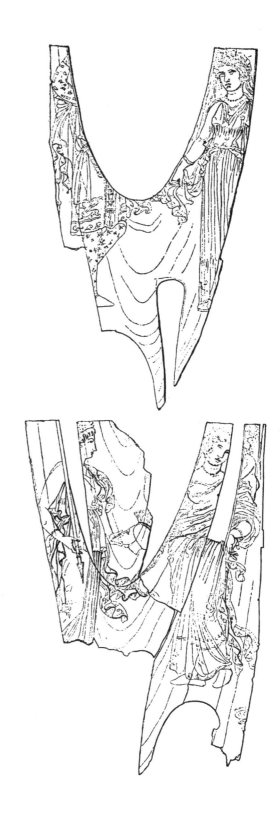

end of the bay so swiftly that the ship nearly ran aground.

First of all they saw to Odysseus. He was still asleep, oblivious to the world, so they carried him ashore in the carpet he had wrapped himself in, and laid him on the grass beneath a tree.

Then they began to unload the cargo.

It was no easy task to carry all those gifts ashore: several heavy chests, a supply of food, jugs of wine, drapes, carpets — all had to be unloaded, while Odysseus slept on soundly.

They found a suitable sheltered spot for him and his possessions, so that no robber might come and steal the sleeping hero's rare gifts.

Throwing one final drape over him, they quickly boarded their ship once more.

They had long set sail again, and perhaps were even close to the island of Scheria, when Odysseus opened his eyes and at last came to his senses.

All this time he had been on his Ithaca, and he had not even known it.

The Wrath of Poseidon

The Phaeacians' ship was still within sight of the last olive on the Ithacan shores, when the lord of the seas and waters, Poseidon, appeared before the throne of Zeus on Olympus.

He was terribly angry, and seethed with rage and fury. He shook his trident, stirred up the waves, and began to shout at his brother:

"Tell me, all-powerful Zeus: what is the meaning of this? Look down from Olympus to Ithaca, and say whom you see there! *Odysseus!* Though he does not know it yet, he has reached his native shores. As though he were guilty of nothing, as though he had not blinded my son Polyphemus, mightiest of the Cyclops! He just lies there, calmly sleeping, and surrounded by gifts. Jewellery,

golden vessels, rare carpets, beautiful material, rings set with precious stones, such as he could not even have brought back as booty from Troy!"

"But Poseidon, Odysseus has suffered so many tribulations, and not once at your hands," Zeus replied, calmly. "He would have drowned, had not . . ."

"And now the mortal Phaeacians! As you see, they have dared bring him safely to the shores of Ithaca! Imagine that, mighty Zeus! I know you decided, when I was away among the Ethiopians, that he would one day see Penelope and Telemachus again. But *one day!* And only after many years of wandering and much hardship, so that he might pay for what he did to Polyphemus — that was *my* decision! Do the plans of the gods mean nothing any more? How will I look in front of the other deities, if mere mortals like the Phaeacians defy my will? I have been dishonoured!"

"But Poseidon, what is this you are saying? How could you, ruler of the seas and shaker of the land, lack honour among the gods?" Zeus calmed his enraged brother. "You are after all the eldest of us, which in itself brings dignity. And there is no need for you to get upset. If you suppose some mortal to have offended you, or even dishonoured you, you have power enough of your own to settle your scores!"

"Then you have no objection to my punishing the Phaeacians?" asked Poseidon. "I should not like to incur your displeasure, ruler of rulers!"

"Do as you see fit. If the Phaeacians have spoiled your plans, punish them so that they may never forget it."

"I should have done so at once, had I not supposed them to be under your protection," Poseidon replied. "But now I will show them what it means to anger me. I will wreak my vengeance on that which is most dear to them!"

"Their ships?" asked Zeus, with dignity, and shifted on his golden throne.

"Indeed, ruler of the clouds, their ships! Their eternal desire to roam the seas! Their constant trips back and forth, carrying men and cargoes! They must bear in mind once and for all that there is a limit to it all. Do you know what I will do? I will change that ship of theirs, in which they are returning from Ithaca, into a motionless rock. And I will raise a tall mountain ridge around their city and port."

"Do as you see fit," Zeus repeated, and without more ado Poseidon descended from Olympus into his watery kingdom . . .

King Alcinous was standing at the harbour wall when the silhouette of the returning ship appeared on the horizon. He and the nobles of his company were already raising their arms to greet the sailors. The ship was in sight; they could already make out the mast and sails. Perhaps some of them were thinking of future voyages, journeys of trade to familiar islands or of discovery to unknown lands. Then, suddenly, they felt the Earth shake beneath their feet. After that a trident could be seen to flash across the surface, and they saw it strike the approaching ship a mighty blow.

The prow, which was lifted by a huge wave, was suddenly left hanging motionless

in the air. The slim masts ceased to rock back and forth, and before the eyes of the astounded Phaeacians there stood not a ship, but a black rock, towering menacingly over the waves.

They stared, dumbfounded and as motionless as that new cliff which jutted from the sea, unable to comprehend what had happened.

It was a long a time before King Alcinous finally spoke, the words catching in his throat.

"Then we have not escaped the old prophesy my dead father feared so much," he said, pointing to the rock, and there was a tight feeling in his breast. "I, too, was afraid that one day the wrath of Poseidon would afflict us ... It was said that he was angry that we guided men safely over the seas, that one day he would destroy our ship, turning it into a motionless rock, and surround our city with mountains. I am afraid we shall have to cease our voyages; the first part of the prophesy has been fulfilled. If we were to provoke Poseidon any further, he would surely throw up mountains all around our city ... Come; we will try to appease the sea god with a rich sacrifice! Bring bulls — the twelve finest animals — and light the sacrificial fires! Perhaps we may yet save our descendants at least from the worst fate which might await them ..."

They obeyed at once.

The flames licked up from their fires, blue smoke climbed skywards, and King Alcinous himself was the first of the Phaeacian nobles to strike a sacrificial bull.

At that moment, on the very tip of Ithaca's headland, the weary traveller Odysseus was starting to stir. He opened his eyes a little, drew his hand across his brow, and looked around him.

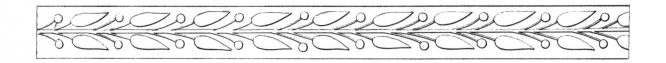

Reunion
with Telemachus

The Awakening

In the first moments after he awoke, Odysseus could not think where he was.

He crawled out of his covers, sat up, and found to his surprise, that instead of the deck of a ship, he was in the soft grass of some corner of a wood. He could hear the rustle of the wind in the trees — they were olive trees. A short distance away he could see a rock, and the entrance to a cave, from where he could make out the pounding of the surf. Where had the Phaeacians set him down? Where was he? Had he not, in the name of Zeus, received a host of gifts from Alcinous? Had they in the end put him ashore on some deserted island and made off with his possessions?

Odysseus leapt to his feet and began to look around him. The chests were hidden in the bushes, and they were all there: inside them were the robes and garments, vases and goblets, jewellery. Many more richer lay beside them. Nothing was missing. He looked around again; he made for the shore, for the cliff which the breakers were striking against, and suddenly saw below him a young shepherd. He was wearing a fine pair of sandals; in his right hand he held a spear, and across his shoulders there was a double blanket. Filled with joy, Odysseus went to meet him.

"Welcome, my friend; I trust you come in peace! Can you tell me something of where I am? Who lives on these cliffs and hills? Is this an island, or some part of the mainland?"

"You must have travelled far, since you ask me so," the young man replied with a smile. "I see from your eyes that the landscape here seems poor to you. But you are mistaken — we have a good harvest of grain; vines grow in abundance, and all manner of fruits. And the cattle of our island are renowned far and wide. Their fame even reached Troy itself, so they say . . ."

"Our *island*, you say?" Odysseus interrupted. "Can you tell me its name?"

"Ithaca, stranger. Ithaca. It is known throughout Greece."

"*Ithaca* . . ." whispered Odysseus, and would have flung himself to the ground to kiss the soil. So this was his Ithaca! It was a little strange — the olive trees had not grown so tall, and the cliffs not been so inaccessible; the paths seemed neglected. Had these hillsides always been so overgrown with grasses and shrubs?

Though he did not recognise his home, he wanted to dance with joy. But he did not wish to demean himself in front of the young stranger. And he thought it unnecessary to betray to the first person he had met in his kingdom who he really was. So he suppressed the cry of joy which was on his lips.

"Ithaca . . . of course," he nodded, and added casually: "I have heard of this island. I do believe it was at Troy, where I served and fought. In fact, I had some small dispute

over the booty from the Trojan war. In the end I came here through Phoenicia. I wanted the Phoenicians to take me to the land of Pylos, but a storm blew up and drove us here. What a tiring journey it has been! We were glad to have dry land beneath our feet once more. I lay down on the ground and fell asleep the moment I got ashore, and the Phoenicians, too. But I am afraid they sailed away without me, though they left all my possessions behind, carrying them ashore for me."

The young shepherd again smiled strangely. It occurred to Odysseus at that moment that the young man's figure, eyes and soft features were those of a woman. He said:

"You have a clever head on those shoulders, and would deceive me! You are indeed no fool, *Odysseus*, and always think of something. Are you surprised that I speak your name? I am not the mortal you take me for, and no fool either. I am Pallas Athene, daughter of Zeus, and your protectress. I came to help you, now that at last you have reached your native soil. You have come home, but it will be no easy task to set things to rights at your court."

This time even the renowned son of Laertes, clever Odysseus, who was always prepared, was left speechless. It was some time before he recovered himself, and bowed courteously to the goddess Athene.

"Noble daughter of Zeus, how was I to know that I was speaking to you! I know you like to take on different guises when you reveal yourself to us mortals, and I know also that you helped us when we fought against Priam at Troy. But since then you have not shown yourself for a long time! And how many times I have almost lost my life! Without Alcinous and his Phaeacians I should not have reached home now — if this really is Ithaca, and not some foreign land!"

"Enough of your sharp words and doubts, Odysseus: you *are* on Ithaca! And do not suppose that I have had an easy time of it with you! You know what you did to the Cyclops Polyphemus — Poseidon is still angry with you. But now you must think how to help your wife, Penelope, and your son, Telemachus. Listen carefully to what I have to say.

"That cave in the rock face that you ran to a moment ago is the home of some water nymphs. They will help you take the gifts which the Phaeacians gave you inside, where they will be quite safe. And then you will be ready to take on all those who are lounging about your house. It will be no easy struggle, for you will find yourself up against a hundred of Penelope's suitors and those who have joined forces with them while you were away. But do not be unduly worried, Odysseus! You know I shall be on your side when you confront them. But now, so that they may not recognise you, I will change the way you look. I will wrinkle your skin, turn your clothes to rags, whiten your hair and take the gleam from your eyes. You will become an ugly old man — a beggar, a tramp. Then you shall go to the shepherd Eumaeus, who has remained faithful to you and loves Penelope and Telemachus. Your son has been good, and has gone to Menelaus in Sparta to seek some news of you. He wants to find out if you are still

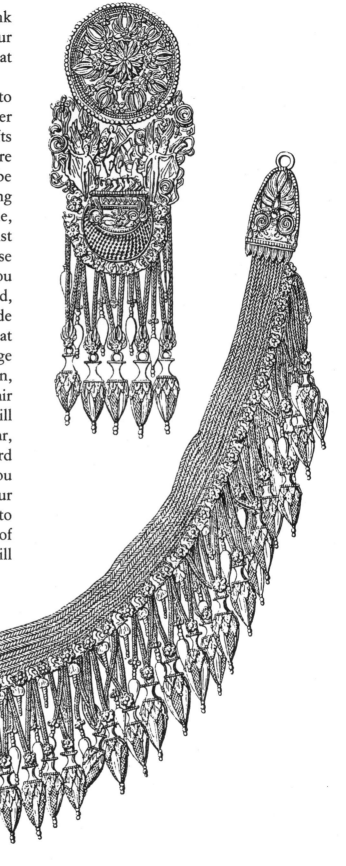

alive. You and he will take your revenge when the time comes."

"My son has set off alone on such a journey? But it is dangerous for him!" cried Odysseus, almost wringing his hands. "I hope the gods will not bring upon him a fate such as mine! Why do you let him wander over sea and land?"

"Have no fear for Telemachus; he is a child no more," Pallas Athene replied. "Anyway, I looked after him throughout his journey to the King of Sparta, and I will continue to protect him — I know his enemies are lying in wait for him. But lose no more time; go and find Eumaeus!"

When she had finished speaking she touched Odysseus with a magic wand.

At that very moment Odysseus' skin grew coarse; his hair turned white and his eyes dull, and his face was covered in wrinkles. There he stood, in a ragged smock, dirty and quite dishevelled, a traveller's staff in his hand. In fact, he was a perfectly ugly old tramp.

Odysseus looked himself over and uncertainly raised his eyes to Pallas Athene. But there was no one there; he was now quite alone on the rocky path.

And he set off up the hill towards the dark forest.

First Night on Ithaca

Odysseus stumbled along the overgrown forest path, then picked his way among fallen stones and pushed through the bushes. The bay was lost from sight when he saw in front of him a more open place, in which there was a courtyard surrounded on all sides by a stone wall. As he drew closer he noted that the wall was reinforced with thick oak posts, and a row of tall, thorny bushes. Around the main building were pigsties; he counted twelve of them, and guessed that each must contain at least fifty hogs or sows.

On the wall sat an old herdsman, cutting leather for new sandals. Around him four large dogs ran backwards and forwards. They

were uneasy, and the moment they saw the tramp they rushed up to meet him.

They growled and barked, and charged at him, and they would perhaps have torn Odysseus to pieces, had not the old herdsman called them off in time. He even had to throw a stone at the fiercest of them.

"They are good watchdogs," he said, as if by way of apology. "They keep watch just as well I do myself. Only they have a master, while I have not seen or heard of mine for many a year. But you need not fear them, traveller . . . You look worn and tired; I daresay you are hungry."

The herdsman motioned to Odysseus to follow him, and he led the way into the house.

He spread some brushwood on the floor and then laid some goatskins on it.

Odysseus thanked him from the bottom of his heart.

"You should rest, and in a while I will fetch a sucking-pig. I cannot offer more than that, for I must give all my fattened pigs to the royal palace," the talkative herdsman went on. "What goings on there are there! Day and night they eat and drink, slaughtering the herds without a care, raiding the storehouses. What those suitors of my mistress, Penelope, don't have served up to them, isn't worth mentioning! She's going from bad to worse, poor thing, like the whole of Ithaca. But what can a humble fellow like myself do about it? I am Eumaeus, an ordinary herdsman, and I have to obey, even if I don't like what I see. If my

master were here, he'd show those good-for-nothings what's what! But the gods alone know what has become of him. He went to join the Trojan War, and has not returned to this day, even though Troy fell years ago."

He sighed, waved his hand, and went out.

Soon he returned with two sucking-pigs; he slit their throats, cut the meat into pieces, roasted them on the spit, and then sprinkled them with barley flour.

He let Odysseus choose the best piece, and brought him some wine.

"I daresay from what you tell me you were very fond of your master," said Odysseus. "What was his name? I have wandered the world for some years; perhaps I have even met him on my travels."

"How many have been here who claimed to have spoken to him! Vagabonds who are ready to think up anything, since they know that Penelope will lend a willing ear, and will reward them. Forgive me for speaking so, but perhaps you, too, would earn a new suit of clothes for some made-up tale."

"But you could tell me the name of your master, could you not?" Odysseus persisted.

"I am almost ashamed to pronounce it, when I know not where his bones may lie. But if you must know, he was called Odysseus. And he was the most just and noble ruler in the world."

"If Odysseus was your master's name," said Odysseus, disguised as the old tramp, "then I can swear by Zeus himself, supreme ruler of men and gods, that he will return home this year. And on all who make themselves at home in his house and dishonour his wife and son he will wreak fearful vengeance."

"I do not believe such prophesies," Eumaeus frowned. "My master will never return! But let us not speak of it, for it always grieves me so! And now I fear for Telemachus. The herdsmen in my charge brought me a message from the city that he has set out for Sparta to ask King Menelaus for help. Somehow that arrogant band of suitors of my mistress found out about it and have sent a ship after him. They wish to settle accounts with him as he returns . . . But we speak only of my master! Tell me something of yourself!"

But Odysseus, not wishing to reveal his identity, as usual made up a suitable story:

"I come from Crete, from a rich family. My father was a wealthy merchant. But I was always more interested in arms, fighting ships and expeditions to foreign lands. I also took part in the Trojan campaign, when the King of Crete, Idomeneus, sent his army against Priam to help the Greek forces. On my way home I had many adventures. In the nine years since the end of the Trojan War there has been much to live through. I would only tell you that when I was in the land of Thesprotia, at the house of King Pheidon, I heard with my own ears news of

your master. Do you know anything of a place called Dodona?"

"But of course," cried the herdsman. "It is the renowned oracle where one can tell by the movement of the branches and leaves of Zeus' oak tree what the future holds."

"Indeed — and your master went there on his journey back to Ithaca, so that he might follow the will of Zeus. I thought I might even see him, but the Thesprotians were travelling to the island of Dulichion, close to Ithaca, and they offered to bring me here. I was glad of the offer — only it turned out to be a trick, for when the time came to land, they suddenly attacked me and robbed me of all my possessions. They even took my clothes, and dressed me in these rags. I was glad when I managed to escape their clutches, and, with the help of the gods, reached this homestead."

"You have told a fine tale," said Eumaeus. "But if it was only to win my favour, then you need not have bothered. I live simply here, among my pigs, and alongside the few herdsmen who help me. But I know what my duty is when someone is in need. And as far as my master is concerned, I do not believe you, anyway."

"How suspicious you are!" laughed Odysseus. "I have a suggestion — let us have a wager on it! If Odysseus returns, I will receive as a gift from you a new suit of clothes, and you will help me get to Dulichion. If he does not return, then you may . . . you may, perhaps, fling me from yonder cliff into the sea!"

"You would lose the wager anyway," Eumaeus supposed. "And to entertain someone and then take his life — Zeus would not approve of that. But we shall see . . . now I must start work, for it is late. My herdsmen will soon be here."

That evening Odysseus helped Eumaeus and his fellows as if he were one of them. It took some time to drive the pigs and sows into their stalls and sties, prepare the swill for the piglets, and clean out the pen. Then the skies clouded over, and there came first a light drizzle, and then a cloudburst, which soon had them all shivering with cold.

"We shall have to make a fire," Eumaeus grunted with annoyance. "I cannot remember such cold weather at this time of year."

They lit a fire, and then they warmed themselves in front of it and talked for a while. Mostly they spoke about how things were on Ithaca, of Penelope, of Telemachus, and the danger they were in. Odysseus added a short tale from the time they fought before the walls of Troy. He told them how he, a Cretan warrior, had once been saved from almost freezing to death by the King of Ithaca's ruse to get him a cloak. He was speaking of himself, of course, but the herdsmen could have no idea that this vagabond in rags was the Ithacan king in person, of whose cleverness he spoke. And they were all pleased at the way he praised their king, for they all liked him well, and remembered him with esteem and love.

Then they made their guest a bed of sheep and goat skins close to the fire, and Eumaeus returned to throw across him his own thick cloak, and to wish him goodnight.

He himself put on an old, well-worn leather coat, picked up the spear which stood in the corner beside the door, whistled to his dogs, and went out to watch over the herds belonging to his master, whom he was sure he would never see again.

The Return of Telemachus

What was Telemachus up to in the meantime?

He counted away impatiently the twelve days he had promised to stay at the house of King Menelaus.

The Spartan ruler enjoyed his company, for it reminded him of the times when he had fought beside his father at Troy. Night after night he held banquets, and each time, at the richly laid table, he would recall those days gone by. When the twelve days were up he tried to persuade Telemachus to stay on, but then he had to admit:

"No, it is not possible. To detain here someone who is hurrying home for pressing reasons is just as out of place as it would be to show a guest the door when he would like to stay longer. I realise that now, Telemachus: you must go, the moment I have had your chariot loaded with gifts for you! Queen Helen will see to it herself."

Each night Telemachus had scarcely been able to sleep, tossing and turning on his bed, unable to stop thinking about what might be happening back at home, how things were going for his mother, what the suitors, anxious to marry her, were up to . . . And on the last night before leaving he did not sleep a wink. After midnight it seemed to him that he saw a figure in the darkness. He recognised her at once by her sparkling eyes.

It was Pallas Athene.

"It is time for you to return, Telemachus," she said to him gravely. "Great events are soon to take place on Ithaca, and you cannot allow the fate of the kingdom to be decided without you. Eurymachus is preparing to force your mother to marry at last. And Antinous is beside himself with rage! But I must warn you — be careful, very careful! Close to the island of Asteris, in the straits between Same and Ithaca, a ship lies in wait for you with your enemies aboard it, led by the ill-tempered Antinous. They want to kill you — stop you returning to your native land. But have no fear! I will send your sails a following wind; but you must pass through at night, and under cover of darkness avoid the place where Antinous and his accomplices are waiting. When you reach the shores of Ithaca, leave your ship and hurry to the solitary home of the herdsman Eumaeus. He is still faithful to you. Stay with him and send a message to your mother by one of the herdsmen, saying you have returned from Pylos. The rest will be clear when you arrive."

As soon as Telemachus heard what his protectress had to say he got up. He woke his friend and guide Peisistratus, son of the

old King of Pylos, Nestor; dragging him out of bed, he told him in a state of great excitement to harness the horses at once and set off.

"In the night?" Peisistratus opened his sleepy eyes wide. "We should break our necks somewhere! Let us wait till morning at least. Then we can load up the gifts from Menelaus, take our leave correctly, and then we can ride like the wind! What is the hurry?"

Telemachus told him what Pallas Athene had revealed.

Peisistratus acknowledged that they must not lose a single hour if it could be helped.

But how long it took to say those formal farewells the next day! How many speeches and toasts there were! How much time was devoted to loading up, under the supervision of Queen Helen herself, supplies of food for the journey, the silver spoon made by Hephaestus himself, the ceremonial robe for Telemachus' future bride, and many other precious things!

It seemed to Telemachus that all this took an eternity.

Everything was ready for their departure, when suddenly an eagle appeared in the sky, carrying in its talons a huge white goose. It descended to their chariot and flew along the right-hand side of their horses.

Telemachus would not even have noticed, but Queen Helen recognised it as a sign of the will of the gods. Just as this eagle had suddenly swept down from the mountains and grabbed a goose fattened in a farmyard, so Odysseus would unexpectedly return, after many hardships, and wreak vengeance on all who had grown fat at his expense and treated his wife and son with dishonour.

"If only Zeus might fulfil this prophesy as soon as possible!"

These were Telemachus' last words as he departed. Then he tugged at the reins and cracked his whip. The ground thundered beneath the blows of the horses' hooves, and a tall cloud of dust rose up behind the chariot.

On the return journey Telemachus did not even stop at the house of King Nestor in Pylos, but Peisistratus understood that his friend was loathe to lose even half a day.

He hurried to his ship as fast as he could, anxious to set sail as soon as possible. To King Nestor he sent greetings and thanks, and vowed eternal friendship to Peisistratus.

They loaded the gifts, raised the mast, hoisted the white sails, and made a sacrifice to Pallas Athene.

No sooner had the land disappeared from view, than they felt a following wind at their backs. On they sailed. And soon they were heading north-west, closer to the shore.

By the time they reached the island of Asteris, in the straits between Same and Ithaca, a dark, starless night had fallen. The ship slipped slowly and cautiously through this perilous place. Darkness protected them from the watchful eyes of their enemies, but they were in constant fear lest they strike some treacherous rocks or run aground in the shallows. It was only when the outline of the Ithacan coast loomed up ahead that they were at last able to breathe a sigh of relief.

By then dawn was breaking.

"Let us make for shore!" Telemachus called out. "Get ready to lower the sails and prepare the ropes! We have managed to avoid the treacherous trap of those abhorrent intruders in Odysseus' house!"

They steered into a quiet bay and lowered the mast, the ship moving along powered only by her oars. Then they dropped anchor and made her fast by her stern. After such an exhausting voyage they needed to renew their strength with a large breakfast before continuing on their way.

When they had finished, they all began to wander down to the ship. They were in their places, the rowers at their oars, and the vessel bobbed up and down in the gentle waves of the bay.

"Telemachus!" someone called. "We're waiting for you!"

But he stood on the bank and waved farewell to them:

"Go on without me, faithful companions! Take my gifts to the palace and tell my mother, Penelope, I have returned! I will come to her, and to you, but first I must go into the mountains to Eumaeus the herdsman."

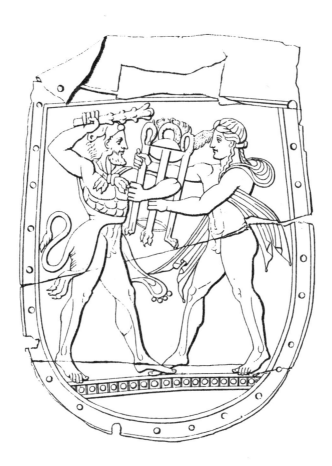

The Reunion

Early that morning Eumaeus, the herdsman, lit a fire and made breakfast for Odysseus. The other herdsmen had already departed with their animals, and the two of them were left alone with the dogs. The latter had already got used to the new guest, even allowing him to stroke and pat them. Now they were lying at the feet of the two men, waiting for some scraps; suddenly, they began to show signs of restlessness. They raised their noses and began to whine and run backwards and forwards nervously.

"That will be someone they know," Eumaeus surmised. "Otherwise they'd be making a proper row!"

In a while they heard footsteps outside and the old herdsman stood up and went out into the porch.

He dropped the bowl he was holding.

"Master! Telemachus! My dear, dear Telemachus! You have come home at last!" he said in a trembling voice. "How afraid I was for your safety, how fearful lest I never see you again! It was good of you to remember old Eumaeus, your faithful herdsman. Come inside and rest; give me your spear, and I will put it in the corner."

As Eumaeus continued to embrace Telemachus and to kiss his hands, Odysseus, disguised as the old tramp, could not take his eyes off the newcomer. So this was his son Telemachus. This was the little boy who used to toddle at his feet!

He could make out in the gentle, still boyish face his mother's features; the figure, neither bulky, imposing, nor on the other hand frail, reminded him of his own youth; the movement with which he handed the spear over to the old herdsman was his, too. But the eyes shone with a brightness that was from Penelope.

He half rose from the seat to make room for the young man.

"Stay there, stranger," Telemachus told him. "See, my good Eumaeus will look after me!"

The old herdsman sat Telemachus down opposite Odysseus, and brought some meat from the previous evening's roast, along with a small basket of bread and a wooden cup of sweet wine.

"This is my guest; he was once a rich man, and comes from Crete," Eumaeus introduced Odysseus. "Yesterday he asked for shelter. He has fallen on bad times . . ."

And he told Telemachus in short the story Odysseus had made up about the Thesprotian sailors. He spoke with obvious sympathy and in conclusion said that Telemachus might perhaps help this

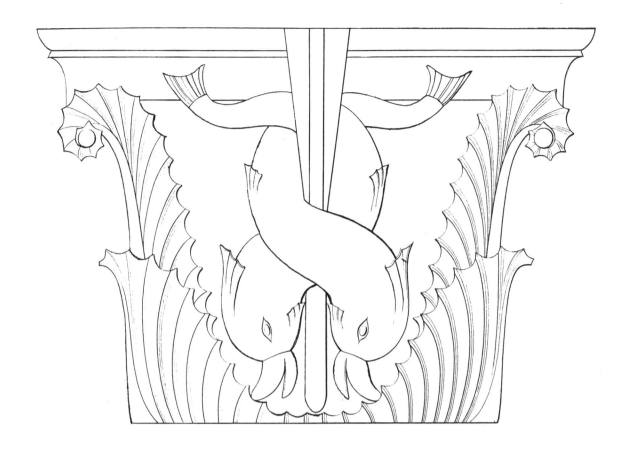

unfortunate fellow — could he not take him to the palace?

"I don't think so, old Eumaeus," Telemachus told him, when the herdsman had finished his tale. "You know what my mother's suitors are like! If I take him there they will start with jests and mockery, and finish with outright insults — and I shall not be able to do anything about it. Indeed, what is one to do, about any of it? But I will help you as much as I can, noble — as I have heard — stranger. I will send you good clothes, new shoes instead of those sandals, and a good, two-edged sword. That should help you on the rest of your journey."

"Young man, do not take ill what I say to you. But when I hear from everyone of the goings on at your mother's court, it makes my blood boil," muttered the old tramp, Odysseus. "Why do you put up with it? Do you want to give way to those arrogant parasites for ever? If I were your age, if I were the son of Odysseus, I should stand up to the whole band of them, and would rather die in combat than see day by day the shame, the mistreatment of guests and hosts alike, the shameless theft, the abuse of the serving-women, the endless drinking-bouts, and who knows what else, of which you complain. Is there no end to their treachery?"

"I see, stranger, that you know a great deal

about what is happening here — but not quite everything. You surely have no idea just how many men pay court to my mother. The lords of Same, Dulichion, Zacynthus — all who have any name at all on Ithaca have moved into the palace and are seeking her hand!"

"And she?" asked Odysseus.

"She cannot resist them, yet she wants none of them," Telemachus replied. "Now even her family say she must make a decision. But she thinks of my father Odysseus still. How it will all end depends more on the will of the gods than on me."

And Telemachus motioned to the old herdsman and said to him:

"Eumaeus, I beg of you, go to the palace to my mother and tell her I am well, and that for the time being I will stay with you in the country. But do not say a word to anyone else! When you have given my message, come back here."

"Should I not tell Laertes, your grandfather, too? They say he was very worried about you when he heard you were leaving for Sparta."

"No — let my mother send someone to him. It will be less conspicuous," Telemachus said. "One of the servant-girls who can be relied on. And be so good as to go at once. I will go with you part of the way."

While Telemachus was accompanying the old herdsman, Pallas Athene appeared to Odysseus. Though Telemachus was not far off, he saw nothing, for the gods appear only to those by whom they wish to be seen. But, strange to say, the dogs must have seen her, for they whined with fear and ran off to the other end of the yard. Pallas Athene touched

Odysseus with a golden wand, and at once his wizened skin grew taught, a fresh colour came to his face, as though he were tanned by the sun, his eyes took on a bright sheen, and his hair and beard were again blond. What was more, the goddess conjured up for him a beautiful suit of clothes and a cloak.

"Go and show yourself to Telemachus, and tell him who you are," she told him. "You shall set off to the palace with him; the day of vengeance is at hand."

When Telemachus suddenly saw in front of him instead of an old tramp in dirty rags a fine figure of a man in noble dress, he thought one of the gods had appeared to him, and he lowered his eyes.

"Be merciful to me, unknown god! I will make a rich sacrifice to you at once, and will bring you gifts. But if I have unwittingly offended you in some way, then forgive me, and spare me your anger!"

"Why do you turn to me as to one of the gods who live on Olympus? I am not one of them, my dear son. I am Odysseus, your father; the one you have always longed to meet again, and for whom you have of late suffered much humiliation."

He embraced his son, and kissed him warmly. Tears of emotion streamed from his eyes.

"You — you are — my father?" stammered Telemachus. "But it is not possible — a moment ago you were a tattered vagabond, and now I see you in all your strength! How can you be my father, Odysseus . . .?"

"My dear Telemachus — however strange it may seem to you, your father has returned home. No other Odysseus will come back to Ithaca. For twenty years I have wandered the world, and have suffered much in that time. But now at last I can clasp you to me; at last I have returned to my native soil! I am different to what I was a moment ago, and different to what I was once. And all is the work of Pallas Athene and her divine power. With her help and on her orders I have come to help you punish those who prey on our household."

"Yes, now I believe that you are my father," sighed Telemachus. "They always told me what a fine, courageous man you were — how wisely you judged. I will take on anything and anyone with you! But we are still only two, and they" — he motioned with his head — "are many. From the island of Dulichion alone there are fifty-two noblemen: there are twenty-four from rocky Same, and twelve come from Ithaca itself. If we go into battle, blood will flow!"

"Which is why, my son, we must be well prepared. I think I know how to arrange it. Tomorrow you will return to the palace; but you will, of course, say nothing of me. Not even to your mother! I will dress as an old tramp again and the faithful Eumaeus will lead me to you. When I arrive, do not allow yourself to be upset, whatever happens. Even if they abuse me and insult me, even if I receive a blow or two, take no notice. I want only to get an idea of just how far things have gone in my house. Wait till I give you the signal, then take all the weapons from the hall to the armoury. Make sure you hide two swords, two lances and two shields somewhere that we may easily find them. That will be enough for us. And that is all I will tell you now. Do not forget that we shall be helped by Pallas Athene herself. All will turn out well, you will see."

"Very well, father," said Telemachus, taking hold of Odysseus' right hand. "All will be well."

He hesitated for a moment, and then added:

"But this evening you must tell me something of yourself. Of how you got to Ithaca. What you said about the Thesprotian sailors was certainly untrue."

"Indeed," laughed Odysseus. "Those Thesprotians were in fact Phaeacians. And I received many gifts from them. Come, I will show you, and I will tell you everything."

Revenge

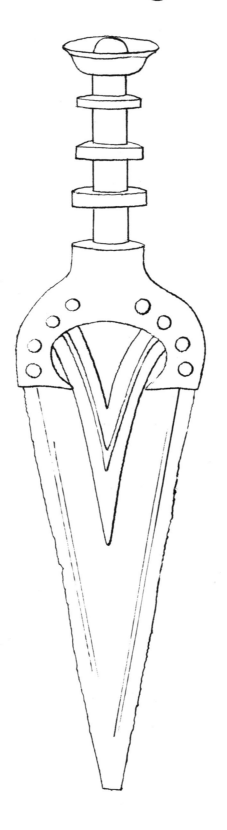

The Suitors' New Schemes

Penelope's suitors were livid.

How could Telemachus have avoided their ambush? How could his ship have escaped disaster?

They held a secret council. The fact that they had failed to get rid of Telemachus filled them with uncertainty, anxiety; but also with anger, and new outbursts of hatred. They must do something!

Antinous, as usual, had the most to say, and as always he was the most uncompromising of them all.

"Make no mistake about it," he ranted, when he had to admit that Telemachus had given them the slip. "He may have escaped us at sea, but he will not be so lucky on land! Whatever happens, he must not be left alive! He's no fool, as he has shown us. If he calls another council he is sure to accuse us publicly of plotting against him. And there's no need to tell you what might await us then — maybe death, or exile for life! There's nothing for it, we must rid ourselves of Telemachus at all costs!"

These were strong words. Some of them, like Eurymachus, agreed passionately, but others were left speechless.

"Perhaps you are right, Antinous," said

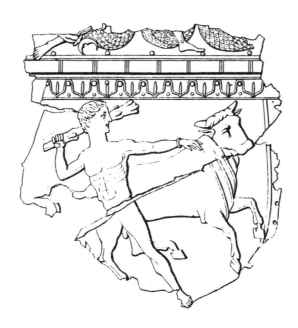

Amphinomous, one of the few suitors who had retained at least a little of his humanity, "but — to kill one of royal blood is a fearful thing. Let us talk it over once more; perhaps we shall think of another way of getting rid of Telemachus, or at least we should try the will of the gods first! If Zeus shows that he has nothing against our plans, then I will agree to what you suggest, and go into battle by your side."

Most of the suitors agreed with what Amphinomous had to say. So the council ended, and they decided to have a banquet prepared.

But one of them, who had already warned Penelope when Telemachus was setting out to visit Nestor and Menelaus, again told the boy's mother of the foul schemes that were being planned to bring down her son.

She ran from her chamber, and as soon as she caught sight of the crowd of suitors pouring into the banqueting hall, began to rail at the cruellest of them:

"Antinous, you villain, you ruffian, do you think I don't know what you are up to? You would take my son's life, would you? Odysseus, my husband, once saved your father's life — and in return you are

seducing his wife, destroying his home, and now you would even slay his son! I warn you — you will pay dearly for it all!"

Antinous was taken aback; for once he could not find a reply. Eurymachus, however, had a ready answer. Though he was himself in favour of making short shrift of Penelope's son, he put on an innocent face.

"O Queen Penelope, surely you are not going to take seriously such slanderous words?" he reassured her. "This is mere gossip! Would I, for instance, who still remember the glorious Odysseus as a boy,

allow any harm to come to his son? We are merely seeking your hand in marriage — and do not forget that it is a matter which must be settled — so we would surely not harm a hair of young Telemachus' head. You may rest assured; do not weep, but go to your chamber and rest."

And he smiled kindly, and even accompanied her part of the way.

But beneath that smile, behind those words of comfort, smouldered a dire, cruel intent.

That night Penelope wept almost without cease. She knew well enough that she should not trust her suitors' honey-coated words.

True, she had received the message from Eumaeus and from Telemachus' companions that her son was alive and well, and back on Ithaca, but what now, when a thousand perils threatened him? In the inhospitable mountains, in the solitary meadows, in the chambers of the palace?

She was therefore beside herself with joy when Telemachus appeared the next day.

She flung herself into his arms, pressing him to her again and again, and saying over and over:

"My son, my dear Telemachus, my only sunshine! How afraid I was that I should never see you again! You left without saying a word! How was your journey? Did you speak to King Nestor? To Menelaus and Helen? Did you learn anything of your father?"

"I was warmly received wherever I went," said Telemachus, trying to calm her down. "They recalled my father with affection, and said what a fine man he was."

"Did they hold out any hope?"

"Menelaus said that on his travels he spoke to the sea-god Proteus, and that he asked about my father."

"And what did the god tell him?"

"I will tell you his very words: 'The lovely nymph Calypso is keeping the Ithacan king prisoner on her island, and he has neither ship nor companions that he might try to escape. He yearns for Ithaca, for his wife and his son. And he is destined to see them again.'"

"Oh that it might be soon! Oh that it might be tomorrow!" cried Penelope. "How I wish our house might be rescued from its dreadful plight!"

Telemachus said nothing.

He could not reveal to his mother that his father had long since left Ogygia, that he had landed on Ithaca, and that he, Telemachus, had spoken to him. Or that the day of vengeance was at hand.

Odysseus, meanwhile, dressed as a beggar and accompanied by the faithful herdsman Eumaeus, was on his way to the city, and to his palace.

Home

After years of longing and near despair, Odysseus again saw his house, his royal home.

Eumaeus, who was accompanying him on the orders of Telemachus, tried to choose the easiest route. He did not really know why he was to take this hapless Cretan to the city, even to the palace itself, when Telemachus had been against the idea at first. He would have been quite glad for the tramp to stay with him; at least he might help look after the pigs, or clean out the sties. Why, then, was young Telemachus sending him to the palace to beg, when he knew well enough how things stood there?

The tramp walked with difficulty, leaning on the staff Eumaeus had lent him; but as they grew nearer their goal, his steps seemed to take on a new liveliness, a new spring. At one moment it seemed to the old herdsman that this unfortunate Cretan knew his way about remarkably well. When they reached the city, he set off in the right direction of his own accord. Then he stopped, clasping the herdsman's hand excitedly.

"So this is the royal palace, Eumaeus? I mean that beautiful building in front of us, with its outbuildings, its tall walls, and its cornices! And those massive double gates! How secure they are: not even the strongest

of men would be able to break them open.
I daresay there is a feast in progress, for I can
smell roast meat from here, and someone is
singing and playing the lute."

"It is like this all the time, these days —
they'll carouse till dawn again. But you are
right — this is the palace where Odysseus
used to live."

They passed through the gates. No one
stopped them; only in the corner by the
wall, lying on a pile of rubbish, a shabby,
sickly-looking dog raised its head. Its coat
was mangy, its body covered in fleas.
Eumaeus expected it to bark at the stranger.
But on the contrary — it struggled to its
feet, and wagged its tail, turning faithful eyes
towards the tramp.

"Arg — my faithful old Arg! He
recognises me even in the form of an ugly
old tramp," thought Odysseus with emotion.
"I brought him up as a puppy — and they
have thrown him out in the dung!"

But out loud he said, as though surprised:

"Look at that dog, Eumaeus. He is old,
but I should say he was of a good family.
How is it that they leave him on the
rubbish-heap? Whom does he belong to?"

"You would do better to ask to whom he
once belonged. To Odysseus, who has surely
perished in some far-off land. He was the
king's dearest dog at the time he went to
fight at Troy — a fine tracker, as swift as the
wind, and as fearless and clever as his
master. Now that he is old, he has a hard
time of it, for no one looks after him. The
servant-girls have no time for him, and there
is no one to tell them their duty."

With these words Eumaeus headed for
the door.

Odysseus could not take his eyes off his

beloved dog. He walked up to him and stroked his back a few times.

The dog raised grateful eyes to him, gave a last whimper of delight, and then hanging his head, he rolled over and died. It was almost as if he had been waiting for this moment for twenty years . . .

They went inside.

The scene in the banqueting hall was a lively one, with dozens of Penelope's suitors sitting at table. Lounging at their head was the insolent and ill-tempered Antinous; the slick and arrogant Eurymachus was strutting up and down, and many other rowdy and ill-mannered types mingled with them. At the very edge of the head table sat Telemachus.

Odysseus, still in the guise of an old tramp, leaned on his staff and stopped in the doorway as if uncertain of himself. But at a signal from Telemachus, Eumaeus came closer.

"Here you are," said Telemachus, and he handed him a basket of wheat bread from the table, along with a good portion of meat. "This is for you, and for the old man who is with you. He is poor; tell him to go round the guests and to ask all of them for some small gift. He would not have the courage to do so himself. But the poor have nothing to be ashamed of."

Odysseus took the food, thanking his benefactor out loud, so that all could hear, and then sat down in the corner by the door, and, spreading the food out, began to eat.

The noise in the hall was quite deafening. The suitors were talking, joking, shouting each other down, roaring with laughter. The musician who played his lute could not be heard above the din.

Odysseus stood up and began to walk round the table. He held in front of him a wooden bowl, and stopped in front of each of the suitors to ask for a gift. They threw money to him, and food, but now and again someone would turn away in disgust, or hold his nose.

"Who is this fellow? Where did he come from? Who brought him here? What sort of ragamuffin is he?" they asked each other, until at last Melantheus, a goatherd, who had long been currying favour with Penelope's suitors, slapped his hand on the table and shouted:

"That fellow Eumaeus brought him from somewhere or other!"

"As if we didn't have enough beggars here," Antinous burst out angrily. "It quite spoils one's appetite. I've half a mind to tear him apart on the spot!"

Odysseus heard him well enough, but he took no notice, and continued his way round the table, holding out his wooden bowl.

By and by he came to Antinous.

"Will you give me some small gift?" Odysseus asked him politely. "You look so noble — like some mighty ruler. You ought to give me more than anyone. Don't think you would lose by it! I should praise your name everywhere I went, and proclaim your magnanimity!"

"Are you going to give me a sermon, or what, you filthy beggar?" spat Antinous. "Get out of my sight!"

"I was not always a beggar, Antinous. I was once a wealthy man; my family was the richest on Crete, and I had everything I could wish for. But I always remembered the poor and needy with some gift or other. And still I lost everything by the will of Zeus, and was fortunate to escape with my bare life from enemies in the far-off land of Egypt."

"What are you telling me all this for — I am not interested!" Antinous raged. "Never in my life have I seen such an insolent old man . . . Be off with you! You'll get nothing from me!"

"There you are, then — you sit at a laden table, bending beneath the weight of the food, and you are not willing to give so much as a grain of salt. And yet the food you have here is not yours to eat!"

It was as if Antinous had been struck a blow. As quick as a flash he reached for a wooden footstool, swung it with all his might, and struck Odysseus in the back.

The tattered old beggar stood his ground, not reeling from the blow, but looking Antinous in the eye; he shook his head, and with his wooden bowl in his hand returned to the corner by the door. Then he picked up his staff and pointed in front of him.

"It is one thing to be wounded in battle; that does not hurt as much as being beaten by the greed of others, by insatiable avarice. But beware, my lords, for even tramps and beggars have their gods and goddesses of vengeance. Antinous, you will soon see! You will leave this world before any wedding is held in this palace!"

"Begone with you!" Antinous screamed, beside himself with rage.

Those who were sitting around him held him back, for at that moment, red with anger, he was reaching for his sword.

"Leave him alone! There's no point!" they told him. "Let us get on with the eating and drinking."

And they again raised their cups, again dangled their fingers for delicacies from the spit-roast heifer. Once more the musician took up his lute, and the banqueting hall rang with laughter and shouting.

Then, all of a sudden, the noise was drowned by the booming voice of one of the revellers:

"Gentlemen, bridegrooms — what a surprise! As if one beggar weren't enough — that scarecrow Irus has come to join our feast!"

A Skirmish with Irus

On the threshold of the banqueting hall stood a skinny young man in rags, and he flew at Odysseus:

"Keep off my path, you mouldy old man! Get out of here before I drag you out with my teeth! Do you hear?" he shouted, in a high-pitched voice.

Though they all knew him as a drinker and glutton, he was as thin as a rake, and as persistent as a gadfly. He was called Arnaeus, but because he was often given messages to carry as he wandered about the city and its surroundings, he was known as Irus — the errand-boy.

"I hear," Odysseus replied calmly, "but I do not see why I should leave, when I have done nothing wrong. If you receive more gifts than I, I will not envy you, and there is room enough for us both. But you must not provoke me, for that would not pay you! I am, you say, a mouldy old man, but I can still show you a thing or two!"

The skinny Irus growled angrily and gritted his teeth.

"How dare you speak to me like that? Watch out that I don't knock your teeth out, you filthy lout! Or do you fancy your chances against me? Come and have a go!"

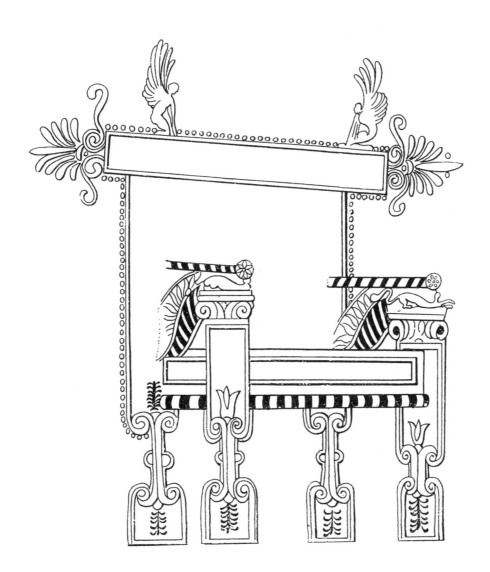

He strode up to Odysseus, and for a moment the two of them stood there motionless, looking each other over sternly.

The suitors were enjoying the quarrel, and Antinous had a great idea.

"Friends, we have never had such a spectacle here!" he boomed to the whole hall. "A fight between two beggars: the gods themselves must have prepared it for us! Go on, you two — get on with it! And what would you say, fellow guests, to a prize for the winner? I'll tell you what: we'll put two goats' stomachs on the fire, and the winner shall choose one of them and eat it. And this evening and in future he shall be our one and only beggar guest. Well, then — is that not worth fighting for?"

"A fine idea, Antinous! Let them fight it out! It'll be good fun!" the suitors called out, the wine having gone to their heads, and at once they formed a ring round the pair of beggars.

"Very well; but no one shall help anyone!" Odysseus agreed, and when the bridegrooms had sworn not to, he began to loosen his ragged clothing.

Suddenly it seemed that it was no wretched old man standing there. How strong the muscles of his legs were! And that huge chest and those broad shoulders! This was not the wispy old man Irus had thought he would put paid to with a single blow! Indeed, he started to tremble, and would have tried to get out of it, had not Antinous yelled at him sternly:

"Why are you suddenly shaking like a leaf, big-mouth? Surely a young fellow like you can still take on an old man . . . Get on with it, or I'll have your nose and ears cut off and thrown to the dogs on the rubbish heap!"

Now Irus really began to tremble with fear, but they were already pushing him into the middle of the circle, towards Odysseus. With wild cries they were encouraging him to begin the fight.

Odysseus watched him, wondering whether to kill him with one blow, or only to disable him and throw him to the ground.

Still, it was Irus who tried to strike first.

He hit Odysseus, but only lightly, and his adversary responded with a blow that sent blood spurting from Irus' mouth. He croaked, staggered, and fell to the ground. Odysseus leapt towards him, and the suitors fell about laughing as he caught hold of his legs and dragged him out through the hallway to the gates. There he propped him up against the wall, shoved a stick in his hand, and cried:

"Now you can squat here and drive away pigs and dogs! And next time leave honest folk alone, or you may come off even worse!"

When he returned, Odysseus sat in his place in the corner by the door, pretending not to notice Antinous, who handed him a goat's stomach and a basket of bread with a smirk. He looked as if he were paying his respects to one who had been victorious over a younger rival, but he grimaced and scowled as he did so.

"You have surprised us; you put paid to that scoundrel in fine style! Now you must hope that you will be as successful next time! And thank you dearly for getting rid of that cheeky glutton! I really don't know what we should have done without you!"

The suitors broke into raucous laughter, and Eurymachus in particular, Antinous' greatest rival, was anxious not to be outdone in mockery.

"I think this fellow was brought to us by the will of the gods," he yelled. "He is surely their darling, for see how wonderfully his skull shines; I daresay there is not a single hair on it! Listen," he said, turning to Odysseus, "I would so like to have you close to me all the time — would you not like to work for me? You might collect brushwood, for instance. You would get enough to eat and clothes for your back. But I don't suppose you are a great one for working . . . You would rather stuff your paunch for nothing!"

"You may make a fool of me if you wish," said Odysseus calmly, not allowing himself to be upset. "But if you must know, you would be surprised to see how I can work in the fields! And if you knew how I can swing a sword in battle, then you would let my paunch be! I suppose you think, Eurymachus, that you are a clever and strong fellow. But if Odysseus were to return, this door would not open quickly enough to let you out, so fast would you run away!"

"You wretch!" shrieked Eurymachus. "Those few drops of wine we gave you out of sympathy must have driven you mad! Or has your victory over Irus gone to your head? You are not going to speak to me like that, and don't you forget it!"

Now it was he who picked up a stool and threw it at Odysseus.

But Odysseus dodged nimbly out of the way, and the stool struck a waiter who was on his way to fill the cups. He dropped the jug, and fell to the floor with a moan. Everyone leapt to their feet, and began to shout at the top of their voices.

"Enough of these games with beggars! Is it worth spoiling our food and drink for them? A pity the fellow didn't choke to death somewhere!"

Telemachus was watching all this from his place at table; quite pale, he stared in front of him and secretly clenched his fists. As he would dearly have liked to throw himself on Antinous, so now he wanted to punish Eurymachus! But he had to put up with these insults to his father — he had promised not to betray anything before the time came, and he had to keep that promise at all costs.

"You do not know what to do with your energy," he called out at least. "You have eaten and drunk too much, and do not know when to stop! Have you not had enough?"

They all stopped dead in their tracks, staring at him in surprise; but then they burst out laughing and called out to him:

"But Telemachus, what is this you are telling us? We have not yet slaked our thirst by any means! Come, waiters, bring wine and fill our cups, so that we may make a libation to the gods and empty all the casks before we go home!"

And they burst out laughing again, and one after the other raised their cups of sweet liquor; to the sound of drinking songs, the carousing went on.

And it went on for a long, long time, late into the night.

Meeting with Penelope

The revels were still in progress when Penelope sent Eumaeus for Odysseus.

The servant-girls had told her of the suitors' rowdy behaviour, and how they kept insulting some unknown guest Eumaeus had brought to the palace. Antinous had first of all struck him with a footstool, and then had thought up the idea of a wrestling match between him and the local beggar Irus. They had all laughed till their sides ached at the thought of this contest, supposing that Irus would be the easy victor, for the stranger was advanced in years. But, strange to relate, Irus had given him just a single blow, and then the old man had struck him so hard in the teeth that he fell bleeding and senseless to the ground! What strength he had for his age! A ragged old tramp, and he hit out like a wrestler! And there was something even more interesting for Penelope: one of the servants said that the stranger had seen Odysseus with his own eyes!

"Are not that rabble of suitors ashamed of themselves, to behave to a guest in that way? They are all repulsive, most of all that fellow Antinous!" cried Penelope indignantly. "I want to speak to that old man. Send Eumaeus for him."

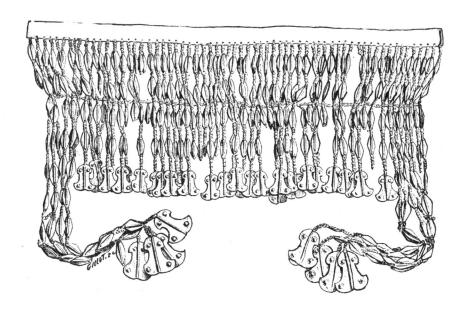

But the faithful old herdsman came back alone.

"Have you not brought him?" Penelope asked disappointedly. "Is he afraid of me? Or too proud? Can he tell me anything of Odysseus?"

"He swore to me that he found some trace of our master at the house of King Pheidon of Thesprotia. He says he is alive and well, and is bringing home rich gifts! Three days and nights he told me of his travels, and a fine storyteller he is, my lady! I am sure you will like to listen to him, too."

"Then why did he not come with you?"

"He begs you to wait until the revels are ended. He says who knows what Antinous and the rest of those scroungers would make of it, were he to come at once."

But evening was drawing near when the debauched suitors finally ate their last morsel, drank their last drop of wine, and with uncertain, faltering steps made their way back to their quarters.

The sound of drunken singing, shouting and wild laughter accompanied them for a long time as they staggered down the street.

Odysseus and Telemachus were left alone in the banqueting hall.

"Dear son, the moment has come for us to make ready our revenge. The first thing we must do is remove all the weapons, lances, helms and shields from the hall. Take them to the armoury, and if they should ask tomorrow why you moved them, say that the smoke from the hearth is not good for them. Come, I will help you carry them. When we have taken them away, you shall go and sleep. Leave me alone for a while; I want to speak to your mother, though

I will not yet reveal to her who I am!"

It did not take them long to move the weapons; it was as though Pallas Athene herself was helping them.

Telemachus said goodnight to his father, and Odysseus stayed on in the banqueting hall alone.

He did not have to go to Penelope; she came to him.

She appeared in the hall with her maidservants, who hurried to the tables to clear up the mess. They collected the remains of the food, wiped the tables and stools, took away the cups, swept up the broken crockery, and carried the bones to the fireplace.

Penelope sat on a couch decorated with silver and ivory. The dancing flames lit her cheeks, and at that instant she seemed to Odysseus as beautiful and as fresh as she had all those years ago when he had left her to join the Trojan expedition.

But she saw in front of her a tramp, a foreigner, who had arrived by some quirk of fate; perhaps the last person who could give her news of her vanished husband.

"I have heard that you know something of Odysseus," she addressed him impatiently. "I should be glad if you would tell me everything you know . . . but before you begin, tell me where you come from."

"Beautiful queen, whose loveliness is renowned far and wide — that is a difficult question indeed. Perhaps it would be better if I were not to tell you at all. I do not have the most pleasant recollections of the past, and then they have given me wine, which makes a man sentimental. Why should I sigh here in vain?"

"Beautiful queen," Penelope echoed, bitterly. "That, stranger, has long not been true. Once, yes, I was beautiful. Once, when Odysseus left for the Trojan war. But could the grief and mourning which have tried me for so long add to my beauty? My suitors drive me to despair, and I scarcely have the strength to resist them any longer. But if Odysseus were to return, then I should get back my freshness again. Tell me where you are from!"

"If it must be . . . I am from Crete, but for many a year I have trekked from city to city. I came into the world in Knossos, where my father was a rich merchant, and I was his second son. They called me Aethon. In Knossos I saw your husband, O queen."

"How did he get there?"

"It was on account of a gale, my lady, which drove him from Cape Malea when he was sailing with the Achaean expedition to Troy. They took refuge on our island of Crete. I myself entertained him and his men for ten — no, eleven or twelve — days, until the sea grew calm and they were able to continue their voyage. We gave them provisions and everything they needed for their journey. And indeed I took part in the campaign myself."

Penelope listened breathlessly to the guest's tale.

Occasionally, as the old man told of how he and Odysseus had together overcome the pitfalls and perils of war, she dug her fingers stiffly into the arms of the couch, or gave a restrained sob. The narrator drew out stories like a conjuror from his sleeve; they were, of course, invented, but they had such a ring of truth to them that in the end Penelope burst into tears.

"But if you knew him so well," she said,

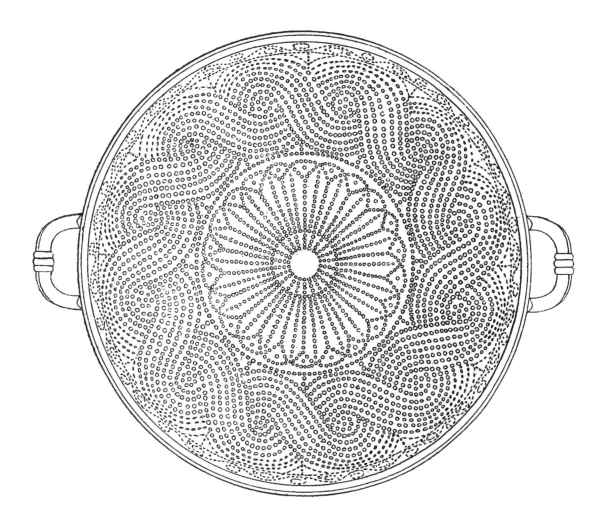

overcoming her sobs, and, despite everything, still suspicious, "tell me what he wore at the time."

This was to be the last test of this mysterious stranger from Crete.

"Queen Penelope," said Odysseus, shaking his head. "It is a score of years ago ... but wait — perhaps I shall remember ... Yes. He wore a purple cloak, with a fancy gold pin. The goldsmith's work was fine and beautiful; I think it showed a fawn trying to escape the fangs of a hunting dog ... In those days Odysseus was accompanied by a friend, an older,

dark-faced man. I remember his splendid curly black hair. Odysseus called him Eurybates, and thought the world of him."

At these words Penelope seemed to curl up into herself.

"My cloak! My golden brooch with the picture of a fawn!" she wailed. "For those were gifts from me, stranger, the only ones I gave him that day when he left for Troy. Now I see that you have truly spoken to him. Gods on Olympus — why have you condemned me never in my life to meet him again!"

She hid her head in her hands, and

her shoulders shook with bitter sobbing.

"Do not weep, my lady," she heard the quiet, soothing voice of her visitor say after a while. "Odysseus will return for certain. True, he lost the ship in which he sailed to conquer Troy, and all his companions drowned in a storm at the hands of Zeus, who punished them. But he was washed ashore, on the islands of the happy Phaeacians, and now lives in Thesprotia. He would surely have returned sooner, but he does not want to come empty-handed; King Pheidon himself told me this. I think you will not wait for him long now. He will return this year — before this moon is out and the new one in."

Penelope dried her tears.

"You have a noble heart, stranger, and wish to comfort me. But I shall never see Odysseus again. I no longer believe it can be so; but thank you for your words. You must be tired. I will tell the servants to prepare a bed for you and to bathe you before they take you to your bedchamber. That way you will be fresh and rested in the morning when you join Telemachus for breakfast."

Now Penelope was quite calm.

"A bedchamber? I am not used to such care . . . Since I have been wandering the world, I have more often slept beneath an open sky than in a comfortable bed," the tramp said, with hesitation in his voice.

"Are you perhaps shy of my maidservants?" Penelope asked with a smile. "Wait — I will call one old woman who used to know my husband. She may at least wash your feet, as is our custom."

She rose from the silver and ivory-ornamented couch and called out:

"Eurycleia! Eurycleia! Come here, my good woman." And she put an arm around the old woman's shoulders. "Wash our guest's feet. It shall be as if you were doing it for Odysseus."

A Scar over the Knee

They went to one side, by the hearth, and there in the shadows Eurycleia prepared to wash Odysseus' feet. She brought a copper bowl, into which she poured cold water from one vessel, and added boiling water from another. She tested it with her elbow to make sure it was not too hot, and then motioned to the guest to lift up the hem of his gown.

Odysseus was afraid. Eurycleia! That thoughtful, kind nurse who had put him to bed, rocked him in her arms, and looked after his things when he was growing up into a young man. He had recognised her at once; he watched her carefully getting ready to wash his feet, and saw her looking at him out of the corner of her eye as she did so. Would she not reveal his secret? As she was accustomed, she spoke as she worked, half to herself, but half addressing her charge:

"Some folk have a hard time of it in this world! If Zeus gets angry, you can offer him the fat meat from the rump every day, and he will still let you wander about like a dog!

Like our poor master, Odysseus. How often I think of him, and how sorry I am for him . . . It wasn't even granted him to bring up his own son. And the insults and foolish words he must have had to put up with — well, our servant-girls didn't speak to you very politely, either, did they? But do you know what, dear guest? The more I look at you the more you remind me of our master Odysseus. You are the same build as he, and have the same voice, the same look in your eye — how like him you are!"

"You have a keen eye, old woman. All who saw us together used to say the same," he replied in a muted voice.

And he shifted a little further into the shadows, until the two of them were scarcely visible; shaking off his sandals, he placed his feet in the warm water.

Perhaps my kind old nurse won't notice; perhaps she has forgotten, he prayed. For it was a long time since, as a boy, he had taken part in a boar hunt in the Parnassus mountains. When their bloodhounds had tracked the creature down it was lying in a den, quite inaccessible through the thicket, almost completely covered with leaves. He could no longer remember if he had wanted to attack it, or if at the last moment the boar itself had got wind of him — but he could vividly remember what happened then: suddenly a pair of savage boar's eyes lit up in front of him. There was a loud fierce snort, and he saw in front of him the snout and the stiff hairs standing up on the boar's shoulders. He lunged at the creature with his lance, but the charging boar had immense strength. It hurled itself at him, and its powerful horns dug into the flesh above his knee, tearing a lump out of it. But

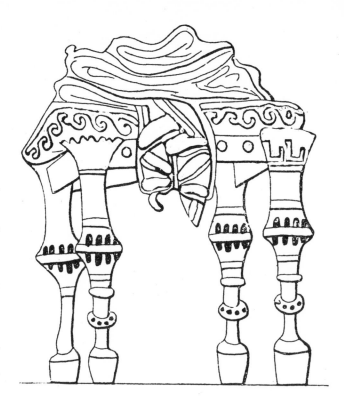

almost at the same instant his lance struck, plunging deep into the creature's right shoulder. It gave a short grunt, then fell to the ground and breathed its last. What a hero he had been! But his nurse Eurycleia had almost fainted when he returned from the hunt with a bandage soaked in fresh blood. She had seen to his wound herself, cleaning and dressing it until it healed. Only a scar had remained, and quite a small one at that.

Suddenly, he felt his calf strike the edge of the basin, and his heel hit the bottom with a thud, sending water splashing out onto the floor.

Eurycleia's palm gently touched the scar, and he heard the faithful old nurse gasp for breath.

● A SCAR OVER THE KNEE ●

"You *are* Odysseus! No one else in the world has a scar like that! How could I have not recognised you, when . . ."

"Shhh! Do you want to destroy me, my dear nurse, whom I have never forgotten?" he hissed. "Yes, I am Odysseus, you have recognised me, and it gives me joy that you did. But I have come to take revenge, and no one in the palace must know that I have returned. Promise that you will be as silent as a stone!"

"I will be as silent as a stone," she vowed, in a trembling, muffled voice. "And when the day of vengeance comes, I will be as strong as iron. But I must tell you that you have many enemies here. Do you know them? I will tell you of them."

"There is no need, Eurycleia. I know enough of them already. I will see to each and every one of them. Leave that to me and to the gods on Olympus."

And Eurycleia asked no more.

She finished washing Odysseus' feet, rubbed them with sweet-smelling ointment, and arranged his ragged garments in such a way that the scar could not be seen.

Then Odysseus took a chair and went back to Penelope, who was sitting thoughtfully on the silver and ivory-ornamented couch.

She stared into space, as if she could see the old tramp no more.

It was as though Pallas Athene had taken her soul off somewhere else for the moment.

"I had a dream," she said suddenly, speaking more to herself than to him. "A

very vivid dream. An eagle flew to the palace, dived down and throttled all the geese. I was sorry for them, and the servants could not comfort me. Then the eagle came back, and spoke in a human voice. The geese are your suitors, it told me, and I am your husband. I have returned to deal out the harsh punishment they deserve. I tried to speak to him, but then I woke up. At once I ran to look in the yard, but the geese were all pecking at the trough as usual."

"The eagle in your dream was right, my lady," said Odysseus. "Your husband *will* return, and none of your detestable wooers will escape his fate. Your dream is an omen."

But Penelope laughed bitterly.

"Not every dream comes true ... And I shall soon have to decide in favour of one of them. But I have just thought of a plan. I will tell it to you. Odysseus used to exercise his agility and skill. He loved one game in particular. He placed twelve axes in a row, drew back his bow, and shot an arrow through all twelve of the axe hooks. And that, my dear old man, shall be a test for all those who seek my hand. Let them try to do as Odysseus did! If one succeeds, it will, I suppose, be the will of the gods, and I will agree to marry him. What do you think to my idea?"

Odysseus bent towards his beloved Penelope, and joy glinted in his eyes.

"You could have thought of nothing better, my lady! And do not delay — before any of your suitors manages to bend Odysseus' bow, your husband will be home!"

"I dare not hope that," Penelope replied, and rose from the couch. The servant-girls were waiting at a distance to take her to her chamber. She motioned to them, and with her head bowed walked away.

Odysseus saw her shoulders shaking with sobs.

Again she would spend the whole night moaning and weeping over her Odysseus.

Before she and her entourage went out of the door, she turned to the old man again:

"Don't forget to say where you want to spend the night. Eurycleia will make you up a bed as you wish."

Axes and a Bow

And the next day it began all over again.

Eurycleia was up and about early, giving instructions to the servants: get a move on, sweep out the banqueting hall, wipe the tables, prepare the plates and cups — the double-handled ones, too. Everything must gleam. The carpets must be beaten, in a minute our lords will be here, and the banquet will begin. Where are the bread baskets? Has Eumaeus arrived with his pigs? What about Melanthius — has he brought the choicest goats? I saw Philoetius bringing a fine heifer — the lords will enjoy that! He's swearing like a trooper, saying they'll bring his herd to ruin; he's right, but . . .

I think I hear voices! Can it be they? They're here, they're stamping on the veranda. What is that they are arguing about so loudly? One of them must be telling jokes! There'll be trouble again today!

As they did every day, the suitors entered the banqueting hall in high spirits. They already had the taste of roast meat in their watering mouths, and of smooth wine on their tongues.

The suitors were throwing their cloaks across the backs of the seats and setting off to see to the slaughter of the best animal, and to decide what should be offered to the gods.

The bread, too, was ready; a deferent Melanthius straightened the baskets, and stood jugs and cups on the table. Penelope's suitors took their places contentedly.

Antinous, Amphinomus, Eurymachus, Ctesippus, Agelaus and the others. And among them, as usual, Telemachus.

Everything was as it had always been; everything was normal. But today *was* different.

Beside the stone threshold of the banqueting hall stood a small table and a chair; on the table were the heart, kidneys and liver of an animal, and beautiful, golden wine. And at this table — on the orders of Telemachus himself — sat the tramp, in his torn smock, his staff propped up behind him in a corner of the wall.

That ragamuffin from the day before! That ruffian who had knocked Irus down!

"What is the meaning of this?"

Eurymachus frowned. "Is this beggar to importune us again at table? Who allowed this?" .

"I told him to sit there," replied Telemachus, in a voice which had a strong, decisive and uncompromising ring. "I told him — be here with us, eat and drink as we do! And if anyone should try to offend you, he shall answer to me for it. After all, this is Odysseus' palace, Odysseus' banqueting hall — and I am Odysseus' son! This man is my guest!"

They were struck dumb, and gazed at each other in amazement. They could scarcely believe their ears.

"You are taking rather a haughty tone with us," said Antinous at last, "but so be it. We are not going to fly at each other's throats over a few words. And above all we won't spoil a good appetite. Let us get on with the business in hand, gentlemen."

And the banquet got under way.

Teeth tore at spit-roast meat; noble wines poured down their throats; greasy chins shone. The suitors smacked their lips with delight, belched, hiccuped, choked over their food and licked their fingers. As the wine started to go to their heads, they grew noisier and noisier, until they were making such a hubbub that they could not hear what each other said.

Suddenly, over that fearful din came the voice of Ctesippus, son of a rich merchant from Same.

"Friends, fellow-suitors," he hiccuped. "I must tell you something. As we have heard, Telemachus has invited a guest. He has given him the same food as us, so he obviously thinks highly of him. But I do not intend to be outdone! I will also give that rare guest a present!"

And he leaned forward, took a great oxbone out of the bone-basket, and before anyone knew it had hurled it with all his strength at Telemachus' guest.

Odysseus only just got out of the way in time.

The wall behind him resounded as the bone struck it.

"Ctesippus, you were lucky," shouted Telemachus. "You were lucky my guest got out of the way, or your rich father might have been preparing a funeral for you instead of a wedding! And, when I think about it, when I see you drinking *my* wine, swallowing beef from *my* ox, and eating bread from *my* grain, I realise what a child I have been till now. But there'll soon be an end to that! I should rather die than look on patiently as . . . for instance, my guests are mistreated!"

When Telemachus had finished speaking there was dead silence.

The suitors frowned and cast hostile glances in the direction of Odysseus' son, but only Agelaus spoke:

"All right, all right, Telemachus. You are somehow out of temper today. But we have told you often anough — it is all your mother's fault. While there was still a chance that Odysseus might return, of course, no one minded that she refused to think of remarrying. But now? None of these things you complain about would be if only Penelope would remarry! Do you know what you ought to do? You should go and persuade her to choose one of us!"

"By Zeus, what are you thinking of, Agelaus? Am I to tell her to do it? Or threaten to throw her out of the house?"

They burst out laughing, but in a few moments the smiles froze on their lips, and were transformed to distorted grimaces; some were so startled that scraps of food caught in their throats. Their eyes popped out of their sockets, and beads of sweat appeared on their foreheads and brows.

In the doorway of the banqueting hall stood Penelope, proudly erect, and she was holding a bow and a quiver full of arrows.

With unspeakable disdain she surveyed the astonished suitors. She had heard everything; she had been standing there for a good while before they noticed her. As she spoke, she spat contempt with every word.

"How many times have you met here now, my wonderful suitors? There have been countless drinking sessions and feasts — what a delightful courtship this is! But I must tell you I intend to put an end to it once and for all. I have decided to leave this house. I will take one of you as my husband, as you keep telling me I should, and he shall be the one who can do what my husband could. Here is a bow and a quiver of arrows. As you can see, the servants have brought a chest from the armoury. In it are twelve battle-axes; in a moment I shall have them set up in a row. The task is as follows: whichever of you can string the bow, load an arrow, and shoot it through the hooks of those twelve axes, as my husband used to do, will take me for his wife. Make ready the axes, please, Telemachus!"

Telemachus cast a glance towards his father, but Odysseus nodded his head to show he was to do as Penelope asked.

So when the servant-girls had opened the lid of the chest, he took out the axes, laid them on the floor, and began to dig a channel in it. It was as straight as a plumbline. He worked fast, very skilfully, and stuck one after another of the axes into the ground, which he then stamped down.

Before long the twelve axes were standing in the ground so precisely and straight that the suitors were filled with awe.

"There you are, gentlemen: all is prepared," he said, breathless from his efforts.

"You heard, gentlemen. All is ready," Penelope repeated.

The suitors were somewhat reticent.

Telemachus picked the bow up and looked around for someone to hand it to.

He would have tried to bend it himself, wishing to show himself to be as strong as his father; but just in time he caught sight of the signal Odysseus gave him: now was the time for the suitors to show their mettle!

Antinous slapped his thighs smartly.

"Come on, then," he called out, with assurance. "Let's say, from left to right, as wine is poured at table. Leiodes will try first!"

"As you wish, Antinous," Leiodes replied, and he took up the bow, turned it a few times in his fingers, and strode over to the doorway to prepare to shoot.

With a sharp movement he tried to bend the bow, until he was red in the face, so much energy did he put into it. The veins stood out on his forehead and his arms, and he wheezed with the effort; but in the end he threw the bow down beside the door, defeated.

"No! I can't do it, however I try! Let someone else have a go!"

"You don't know how to use a bow," said Antinous, disparagingly. "First you must prepare your weapon. Servants — bring me a piece of lard!"

When they brought it, Antinous picked up the bow and took it to the fireplace; he ordered Melanthius to get it smoking well, and then warmed the bow over the fire and rubbed it thoroughly with lard.

"It will take a while, but then you'll see," he said, boastfully. "Now whose turn is it? Eurymachus!"

The latter grinned, sure of himself; he seemed to think Leiodes unskilful — it could not be that difficult to string a bow!

He looked around the suitors, and with a gesture of confidence spread his legs and began to pull on the string. In a little while it had dug into his hand, and a bloody line appeared on his swollen skin. He cast away the bow, which Eumaeus just managed to catch, and, angrily inspecting his wound, cried out:

"It's not possible to shoot with this bow! Was Odysseus an Olympian god, that he was able to string it? Penelope is not worth so much to me that I should tear my flesh on account of her stupid ideas!"

"If Eurymachus can't do it, then I can!" cried Amphinomus, and was in such a hurry to grab the weapon that he nearly fell flat on his face.

But he did no better.

After that Medon, too, tried in vain, followed by Agelaus, and after him the loud-mouthed Ctesippus was a dismal failure, too. None of them was able to string the bow, lard or no lard, until at last Antinous' turn came.

Odysseus smiled: the hour of vengeance was at hand.

When he had seen the suitors struggling vainly with his bow, he had taken aside for a moment the head herdsman Eumaeus and the cowherd Philoetius, whom he had heard cursing the suitors that morning for taking away the finest of his animals. Who was to put up with it, he had said — if Odysseus were there, he'd soon show them what was what! Now both the herdsmen were watching with disgust the endless frolics of Penelope's wooers.

The old tramp addressed the two of them intimately:

"Friends, I know well that many things here are not to your liking. Perhaps I should keep quiet, but I will let you into a secret. If, perhaps at this very moment, let us say by the will of the gods, Odysseus were to

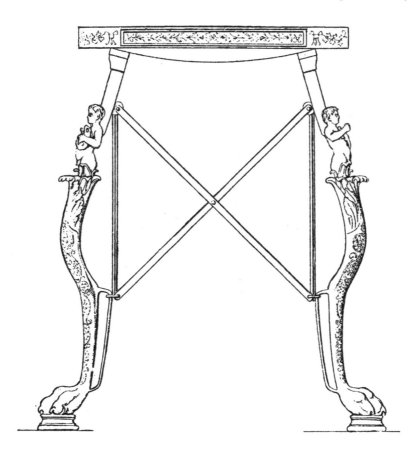

appear before you and wished to deal with these intruders in his house — would you lend a helping hand?"

"How can you ask, old man? Then these bridegrooms would soon see what my muscles can do," Philoetius replied, and Eumaeus lent his voice, too:

"Have I not called daily on the gods of Olympus to send him back to us? If only he were here already!"

Odysseus squeezed their shoulders firmly, drew up the hem of his ragged garments, and showed them the scar over his knee.

"That which you have longed for is come to pass. *I* am Odysseus; I have returned after twenty long years; so that you may be sure, look here. Do you recognise the scar left by the wild boar in the Parnassus mountains?"

"Odysseus!" they both gasped, when they saw the scar, and would have embraced him on the spot.

He had to restrain them before it was too late.

"I see that you welcome me here, and wish to stand by me faithfully," he said. "But for the moment we must not reveal ourselves. Listen what we must do. First of all close the servant-girls' chamber door and shoot the bolt. None of them must come out, however much clamour and din they hear from the banqueting hall. Eurycleia will help you with that! And the main gates must also be locked — you see to that, Philoetius. In the meantime, I will ask them to lend me the bow, so that I may try to bend it. When my arrow has flown through the hooks of

those twelve axes, I will wreak vengeance on these disgusting intruders. Now, let us get on with it!"

At that moment Antinous' turn came. Though at first he had been sure that he could perform Penelope's task without any trouble, now he was not the least bit inclined to try his luck.

He was afraid he would fail, that he would not be capable of bending the bow, and wished to avoid such humiliation if he could.

"I think we should stop playing these games," he suddenly suggested. "Today all are celebrating the feast of Phoebus, and we are standing around trying to draw an old bow! Perhaps that is why none has been able to do so. It would be wiser to offer a sacrifice

to Phoebus and pay tribute to him, like the rest of the Ithacans. There will be time enough for archery contests tomorrow."

The suitors liked Antinous' idea: what they had not succeeded in today, they might be able to do another day! With a subdued murmuring they began to go their separate ways.

But the hum of voices was suddenly cut through by the voice of Odysseus.

"A sensible suggestion, my lords, guests in this house! It would be as well to do as Antinous suggests. But before you do so, allow me to try out how much strength I have left in me from my youth. I was once able to bend any bow ... though I am no longer the man I was."

"You must have gone mad, or you are

drunk!" snapped Antinous. "Be glad you may stay here with us, among noblemen, and eat and drink in the same room, hear our conversation, though you are just a tramp! Or would you like to enter the contest for Penelope? What would the noble lady say to that?"

And he turned to her as if seeking confirmation of what he said.

Penelope, running a glance over her suitors, replied:

"Above all, he is Telemachus' guest, and should not therefore be slighted in any way. Or are you afraid that he will be able to draw the bow and shoot through the axes? That he will take me home as his wife?"

"We are afraid of slander and gossip, Penelope," cried Eurymachus. "Lest they say that some beggar sneaked into the first house of the land and won in an archery contest a bride from the noble line of Icarus!"

"But he, too, I believe, comes from a noble and rich family. He has been the victim of fate," Penelope replied. "Give him the bow; we shall see with our own eyes what he can do."

"All this is a matter for us men," Telemachus broke decisively into the discussion. "Leave these matters to me, mother, and go to your chamber to rest."

She looked at him in wonder — could this be her Telemachus speaking? Where did that bold, resolute tone come from? This was the voice of a man, and not of the youth who had almost been overlooked in this house until now.

Her astonishment turned to pride. She rose, and with an unhurried, dignified step left the banqueting hall.

"Eumaeus!" called Telemachus, when his mother had disappeared through the doorway. "Hand my guest the bow!"

Odysseus got to his feet, left his place in the corner of the hall, and took the bow and quiver from the herdsman. He strode past the row of twelve axes, surveying them intently. Then he bowed his head and examined his weapon closely: he tested the wood, afraid that over the long years woodworm might have eaten it. He turned it round in his hand from side to side, scrutinising it inch by inch.

"He's looking it over as if he were buying a cow," quipped one of the onlooking suitors.

"The old man must have one like it at home!" added another.

But Odysseus took no notice of jokes and jibes. He did not even react when a number of the spectators began to laugh raucously.

He took an arrow from the quiver and placed it on the table. Then he put one foot on a chair, felt for the groove at the end of the bow, and slowly began to bend it.

The heavy wooden frame arched inwards.

Odysseus nimbly slipped the bowstring into its groove, made it fast, and tried it with his finger and thumb. There was a satisfying twang, like the voice of a swallow.

He drew the bowstring back a little and then let it go, and the beautiful sound was heard again.

And at that moment, when not a breath could be heard in the banqueting hall, almighty Zeus himself gave Odysseus the signal, with a huge clap of thunder, that the moment of revenge had arrived.

Odysseus picked up the arrow and set it in the bow; his left hand held its body rock steady, while his right drew back the string slowly but firmly. For an instant he closed one eye and took aim. Then he loosed the grip of his fingers, and the heavy metal arrow whizzed through the air and shot through all twelve axe hooks.

At that moment none of the suitors could move a muscle. Then one of them cried in a voice filled with awe:

"He's shot straight through all twelve holes!"

And, at the other end of the banqueting hall, Odysseus' rebounding arrow rattled, jumped and spun across the floor.

Revenge

"That foreign tramp didn't make a fool of himself, did he, Telemachus? He had a stronger arm than all those who insulted him, abused him and made fun of him!"

Odysseus was holding the bow in his left hand, watching the bouncing arrow, and with his right hand straightening the quiver. He pointed to the suitors, still standing as motionless as statues, and fingered the feathers meaningfully.

"And now, son of Odysseus, we should hold a pleasant supper for these lords. There will be time enough for entertainment afterwards!"

Telemachus understood.

He hurried into the alcove where he had hidden the weapons, and in a flash was standing by Odysseus' side, sword belted at his waist, lance in hand.

At the same moment Odysseus flung aside his tattered robe, and with a sudden movement emptied the arrows from the quiver at his feet. He placed one of them in the bow. Standing in the doorway of the

banqueting hall, he turned his fierce gaze on every one of them in turn.

"Your innocent entertainment is over," he thundered. "Now there will be another target, and with the aid of Apollo I trust I will hit it!"

Antinous, pale with fear, reached for his goblet of wine. With trembling fingers he raised the two-handled gold cup to his lips.

Odysseus drew the bow once more. His deadly arrow swished.

The cup fell from Antinous' fingers, rang against the tabletop, and rolled onto the floor. The arrogant and ill-tempered Antinous, son of the lord Eupeithes whose life Odysseus had once saved, clutched at the arrow lodged in his throat. He started a little, and grasped the table stiffly, knocking off cups and plates. Blood spurted from his throat, mixing with the wine and food.

The suitors were filled with horror.

"What's going on? The fellow is shooting at us! Cut him down! To arms! Swords! Lances! Bows and arrows!" the shouts rang through the hall. In confusion, they ran hither and thither, looking for their weapons.

But the arms which the revellers had left standing there were safely locked in the armoury.

● REVENGE ●

203

And among the shouting and the cursing, the pleas, accusations and lamentations of the suitors, Odysseus' mighty voice boomed:

"You dogs! You thought I should never return from Troy! You made my house into your lair! Now I stand here before you — I, *Odysseus*! And every last one of you will pay for what you have done here. Not one of you will escape his doom!"

"Odysseus has returned, Odysseus is here!" came the terrified shouts, and the panic among the suitors grew by the instant.

"But you have already punished the one who was the cause of it all," piped Eurymachus, in great fear of his life. "It was all Antinous' fault! He was the one who was most to blame! He wanted to be King of Ithaca, and he even wanted to slay your son! You were right to punish him; we admit it, and we will repay you the damage we have caused you. You shall have cattle, gold — a huge recompense from us . . ."

But Odysseus did not even let him finish speaking.

"Even if you gave me all you property, Eurymachus, it would not save you from my wrath! You have only two choices: to fight, or to run away — if you can!"

"Then we will fight!" cried Eurymachus.

And a fearful struggle broke loose.

Odysseus felled Eurymachus with a well-aimed arrow; Telemachus drove his sword into Amphinomus; arrows whistled, and swords crashed. The faithful herdsmen Eumaeus and Philoetius hurried to Odyssues' aid. But in the confusion, the bitter hand-to-hand struggle, no one noticed the treacherous goatherd Melanthius slip into the armoury and bring arms for their enemies.

Now the fight was even crueller than before.

On one side there were Odysseus and Telemachus and a handful of faithful friends, on the other a crowd of angry and desperate suitors, who knew they could expect no mercy. The battle was bitter and bloody, for the foes were fighting for their lives.

Hair matted with sweat, blinded with fear, they fought without respite. The banqueting hall resounded with groans; blood stained the floor, and the bodies of those slain by Odysseus' arrows or Telemachus' sword lay among the tables, on the chairs and on the ground.

Ctesippus had already fallen to a blow from Philoetius; Agelaus slumped with a sword wound deep into his throat. The end of the treacherous herdsman Melanthius was especially cruel. Leiodes, too, died at Odysseus' hands, and the bloody battle went on.

Odysseus, Telemachus and their companions would scarcely have escaped with their lives against such odds, had not Pallas Athene herself come to their aid at the last moment, when they were at the end of their strength. With her divine power she turned aside the arrows aimed at Odysseus and his faithful ones, broke the lances which lunged at their breasts, and parried the blows of swords.

The fearful struggle went on for a long, long time.

Only Medon's life was saved, since he had refused to join the plot against Telemachus' life, along with Phemius, who had entertained Penelope's suitors with his lute and his songs, but only because he was made to do so by force and violent threats.

Then the last of Odysseus' enemies had fallen.

The last arrow had whistled from the great bow, the last sword thrust had been made, and for the last time blood spurted from a wound and the last death rattle echoed through the hall.

A terrible silence fell.

Odysseus lowered his bow, and Telemachus rested his hand and his sword on the table. The Ithacan king ran his eyes up and down the quiet banqueting hall . . .

Yes, all those who had wronged him, his wife and his son were there. None had escaped terrible punishment. They lay there like fish cast out of a net onto the shore.

Odysseus kicked away the cloak of one of those who lay lifeless at his feet. He cast aside his bow, looked round for Telemachus, who was so exhausted from the battle that he could scarcely stand, and held out both hands to him.

"Our vengeance is accomplished," he said.

He picked up a cup from the table and quenched his thirst. Then he turned again to his son.

"Let the servants clear up here. Telemachus, see to it, please. But those who served my enemies must be duly punished — see to that, too. And send Eurycleia to me!"

The old nurse was not long in coming. She hurried up at once, radiant with joy, and with a deep bow stood before Odysseus.

"At last you have delivered us from those villainous rogues, my lord! They have only reaped what they sowed — what they have been sowing for years. I am ready to obey your commands, my dear lord. Am I to prepare you a bath and clean clothes?"

She had read in his eyes the tiredness and complete exhaustion.

He nodded, and gently stroked her grey, thinning hair.

"Yes," he assented, wearily. "And tell Penelope I am here; that I have returned."

Penelope's Test

Penelope could not believe the old nurse's news. Why had Eurycleia woken her up on with such an unlikely story? Wherever had she heard it? Odysseus had returned? He had defeated all her suitors in a cruel battle? Antinous, Eurymachus, Ctesippus and the others were lying dead in the banqueting hall? Telemachus had also ordered harsh punishment for those of the servants who had thrown in their lot with those shameless intruders?

"Do you wish to mock me, Eurycleia? If it were not for your years I should be most angry with you!" Penelope replied crossly, still half-asleep.

"But our master has indeed returned, my lady," Odysseus' old nurse insisted. "He is that tramp, that beggar, whom they all laughed at; he who came to visit you. I saw him in the banqueting hall with my own eyes, standing like a lion amidst those dead scoundrels. The shouting could be heard from the servants' quarters, but whoever would have imagined such a battle was raging! The gods themselves must have helped our master and Telemachus against such odds . . . He has given orders for the whole house to be set to rights, for the bodies to be burnt, and for all signs of the battle to be removed. And he sent me to tell you that he has returned."

But Penelope would still not believe it. However much Eurycleia tried to persuade her, even though she spoke of the scar she had seen, Penelope could not believe that the impossible had happened.

Even when she entered the banqueting hall and saw him sitting beside a tall pillar, staring into space, she was still not sure.

Now she seemed to recognise the features

of his face, the mouth, the lips, the brow of Odysseus; but in a moment they again seemed unfamiliar to her, as if they belonged to a total stranger.

She sat down in a chair by the wall opposite him, and folded her hands on her lap. Minutes passed, and she could not utter a word.

"Mother, why do you not speak? My father, your husband, has returned to us. Will you not even welcome him?" Telemachus broke the heavy silence. "After so many years . . . and you will not even embrace him?"

"It is all a little too much for me, my son," Penelope replied. "I scarcely know what to say, and I am almost afraid to look this person in the face who has come as Odysseus. Is it he, or is it not? But if it is truly Odysseus sitting here before me, I shall soon know."

"Can you be serious, Mother?" Telemachus asked incredulously. "Is it not enough that he has dealt with Antinous, Eurymachus and the other scroungers on our household? Have you a heart of stone?"

At this Odysseus intervened. "Be calm, Telemachus. I understand how your mother feels. I understand that she wishes to be quite sure after all these years. And I am probably not a very pretty sight after that bloody fray. But I shall soon convince her . . . Now listen to me! We will all meet at a feast to celebrate these events. I want today to be merry! Tell everyone to wear their best clothes; there will be music, singing and dancing, as if a wedding were being celebrated!"

The whole of Odysseus' palace soon resounded with singing and playing.

The young people danced and rejoiced, the older people sang: the women wore their finest robes, and the singer Phemius

accompanied the celebrations with his most touching songs.

Odysseus, washed, his hair carefully combed, made his appearance in a new robe among the merrymaking Ithacans and sat down on the couch beside Penelope. They listened to Phemius' lute and drank sweet, chilled wine, and both thought about the days to come.

"Is it not cruel, Penelope, that you behave towards me with such reserve? As if you had a heart of ice?" Odysseus said later on. "Will you have a bed made up for me?"

This was the moment Penelope had been waiting for.

It was to prove conclusively whether the man beside her on the couch was indeed Odysseus.

"Eurycleia will see to it," she replied, and at once she gave orders to her faithful servant:

"Have Odysseus' bed taken out of the bedchamber, and tell them to lay blankets and carpets on it."

At these words Odysseus frowned; his hackles were raised, and, filled with indignation, he cried:

"What is this you say, Penelope? Has anyone the strength to move my bed? Why, I remember how I made it! That time, years ago, there was an olive tree growing in the garden. With my own hands I stripped its branches and hewed its trunk to make the pillar for our bed. Only then did I decorate the bed with gold and silver and carvings in ivory. And when all that was done, I made the wall of our bedchamber, and last of all the door ... How could anyone move that bed of ours, unless they cut off that olive trunk! Or has that already been done?"

This time even the clever, sharp-witted Odysseus had not seen through the trap.

So his annoyance was not feigned, his indignation was real.

But Penelope felt her heart beat faster, and her knees quiver.

Tears of joy rose to her eyes; she threw herself upon Odysseus and embraced him; sobbing, she stroked his hair and showered

kisses on his cheeks, his lips and his eyes.

"Do not be angry with me, Odysseus, my dear, clever, wise husband, over this little test! Now I believe you; now I know that it is you! No one beside the two of us could have known the things you have told me. For so long the gods sent us nothing but tribulations, and did not allow us to spend the years of our youth together, to grow old side by side. Do not be angry with me for receiving you so coldly, but I was afraid I might be disappointed, or deceived. But now you have convinced me. Now I am yours."

It was like when a ship, battered by storms and angry seas, comes within sight of land, and safety. Like when a swimmer eludes fearful dangers and finally steps ashore on dry land.

For a long time Odysseus embraced Penelope, for a long time Penelope held Odysseus to her breast, and they clutched each other tight.

"Come," Odysseus said. "Night is falling."

"Your bed is prepared," said Penelope. "Tonight, and whenever you please . . . Will you tell me of what you have endured during these long years of parting?"

Eurynome, Penelope's good and faithful chambermaid, lit the way to their bedchamber. The noise of music and dancing in the banqueting hall was left far behind them, and Phemius' lute sounded only faintly.

They sat on the bed, with its soft coverings, and Odysseus began his tale. He told of how he and his twelve ships had left the conquered Troy. Of the battles with the Cicones, and of the land of the Lotus-eaters, whose food brings forgetfulness. He recounted the incidents with the one-eyed Cyclops Polyphemus, and the fearful giants, the Laestrygones.

He told of Circe, the lovely enchantress, who changed men into hairy pigs, and how on her suggestion he had entered the underworld and spoken to the seer Tiresias, and with the spirits of the dead. Then he spoke of Scylla and Charybdis, through whose snares he had to sail twice. And of the nymph Calypso, who tried to persuade him to stay with her, offering him immortality and eternal youth.

And in the end he told her of kind King Alcinous and the Phaeacians, who had brought him to Ithaca, giving him many rare gifts.

Penelope, too, had much to tell. Odysseus heard of the humiliation and insults she had had to suffer, how the arrogant suitors had laid waste his estates, and how things had gone so far that they plotted against Telemachus' life.

One night was not enough for all these

recollections, nor for the words of love and countless embraces that Odysseus and Penelope exchanged . . .

But the kind Pallas Athene held back Eos, goddess of the morning light, and delayed her pink chariot, to which the two young horses Light and Brightness are harnessed. It was not for a long time that the dawn at last filled the bedchamber with daylight.

When they awoke, they were ecstatically happy. For in the night the goddess Athene had given them back their youth.

Reunion with his Father

After a long night filled with happiness and love, the first to wake was Penelope.

In that late dawn she leaned over her beloved spouse and gently touched his hair, his eyelids, his lips.

"My lord, my dear husband Odysseus, do you know that the lovely goddess with rosy fingers, Helios' sister Eos, has emerged from Oceanus to pour her clear light over the heavenly globe? I am so happy that yesterday was no mere dream, to dissolve with the coming of the dawn! And I am happy that the war which tore you away from me for so long has ended, and that my Odysseus will never again have to leave me with weapons in his hand. And that our days to´come will melt away in happiness and in peace, now that the good gods have returned our youth to us!"

"And have we not suffered many a dire moment through their will?" Odysseus replied, embracing his wife and giving her a kiss. "You, who have suffered for me at home, and I, who have had to overcome one obstacle after another in my long journey back to my native Ithaca. You are right: we shall never part again, but shall be together for ever, and rebuild together what those arrogant suitors of yours have destroyed. But now, my dear, take all your servants and hide in the upper chambers of the palace, and do not show yourself to anyone! When the news gets round the city of how I dealt with those who ravaged our kingdom,

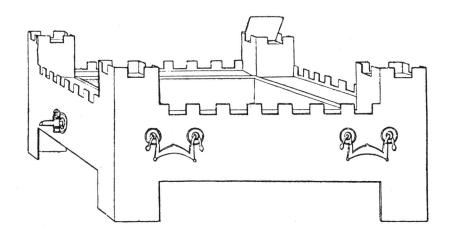

anything might happen! For I still have one duty to fulfil, and that is to visit my old father on his farm. He surely pines for me, the poor fellow, and has perhaps given up all hope of seeing his son again."

Once again Odysseus embraced Penelope and covered her face with kisses. Then he sent for Telemachus, gathered a few of the herdsmen together for the journey, and told them all to take lances, swords and shields.

They set off together out of the city, down onto the plain where Laertes had long ago departed to his farmstead out of sheer grief. He had a comfortable home there, with an old woman from Sicily as his housekeeper, and the needs of the farm were seen to by his faithful servant Dolius and his six sons, who lived in a house nearby. It was to this building that Odysseus sent his escort, led by Telemachus, with orders to slaughter a pig and make ready a meal to celebrate his return.

After so many years he wished to meet his father alone.

He did not find him among the vines, which was the first place he looked, but in the beautifully-kept orchard, where the old man was digging round an apple tree. His heart sank when he saw his father in a soiled, patched smock, with a worn-out goatskin cap and oxhide boots which, though often mended, were still full of holes.

He stopped in front of a tall pear tree, and for a while fought back his tears, not knowing what to do. His first instinct was to

run to his father, embrace him, and reveal his identity at once. But then he decided to act otherwise. No, it would be better to prepare his father for the joyful news!

So he went up to the old man, who was still busy turning over the soil, and did not seem to notice anything or anyone around him. Putting a hand lightly on his father's shoulder, he said to him:

"Greetings, old man, and I wish you success in your labour! I see you work hard, for your apple trees are in fine shape. And the olives, figs and vines are a delight to behold! Every tree is a witness to the care you take of your orchard. But you do not look after yourself quite so well! Are those patched and neglected clothes your own? It is not your fault to be sure, for at your age you should have someone to look after you. Whose gardener are you, that they let you go about in such rags? But forgive me for speaking so; in fact I only wanted to ask if I am on Ithacan soil. I met some fellow on the way, who said it was so, but I couldn't get much sense out of him . . ."

At last the old man raised his head from his work.

"Are you looking for someone?"

"An old friend. He was once my guest. A fine fellow — I took a liking to him, and I should like to see him again. He said he was from Ithaca, that his father was Laertes of the house of Arceisius, and that he was himself King of Ithaca, whom ill fortune had carried far from his native land. Indeed, I entertained him right royally, and gave him

many gifts for the journey." The old man nodded his head with emotion.

"You are indeed on Ithaca, stranger, but times have changed! Now there is no ruler here from the house of Arceisius, but a rabble of usurpers! If you were able to find your guest, or, as you say, friend, here, then be assured that he would repay richly all you did for him. But the gods alone know where he has got to . . . Tell me something about him — how long is it since he stayed with you? A year? Five? Or still longer? I should like you to tell me the truth, for — you should know — I am Laertes, his father, and I have been waiting for him for many long years!"

The old man stopped in his tracks, fixing Odysseus with a searching expression.

"But tell me who you are! Of what house are you? And where have you come from? Did you come by your own ship, or have they set you ashore like a wayfarer?"

"Who am I . . . ?" Odysseus replied, after a moment's silence. "My name is Eperitus, and I come from the city of Alybas, where my father has a beautiful palace . . ."

Once more, as so many times before, Odysseus wished to make up a fine tale about himself, but this time his voice wavered.

"I must have come here by the will of the gods . . . the wind blew my ship to these shores, perhaps so that I might meet my friend . . . It is five years since he left us in Alybas . . . But he left accompanied by most favourable omens, and so we both hoped to meet again in friendship."

The words came to Odysseus only with great difficulty. He could not finish his sentences, and as he, always so eloquent, stammered and stuttered, beads of sweat broke out on his brow. And when he saw Laertes pick up a handful of dirt and sprinkle it on his grey head with a loud groaning, he felt as if his heart would break.

No, he could stand it no longer!

He leapt towards his father and embraced him, then fell to his knees and covered his wrinkled hands in kisses.

"Father, dear father," he cried, sobbing with joy, "*I* am your son Odysseus, *I* have returned after so many years, to you and to Penelope! Do you not recognise me? Look

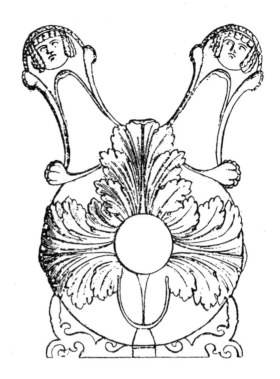

at the scar left by that boar's horn on Mount Parnassus. It was you and mother who sent me to grandfather Autolycus for gifts, that time — do you remember? And I can show you the trees here in the orchard which you gave me as a boy — those thirteen pear trees and ten apple trees, and forty figs! And you promised me you would give me fifty rows of vines, each maturing at a different time. Who else could know this but your son? Father, do you now believe that I am Odysseus?"

For a long while Laertes was unable to say a word. He could not see for tears, and only embraced his son again and again, and listened with emotion to the story of his wanderings, of his meeting with Penelope, and of how he had defeated that villainous band of wooers in the royal palace. At that

moment lines of anxiety and worry creased his forehead. Would not the friends and relations of the suitors wish to take a quick revenge for their punishment? Was Odysseus not in new danger? Would cruel fate not tear him away again at the very moment he had returned, after twenty years away from home?

"Drive all such thoughts from your mind," Odysseus reassured him. "Now we will go into your house and celebrate our reunion as befits. Telemachus and my herdsmen have surely prepared a feast. We can look forward to roast lamb and cups of wine!"

"And grateful sacrifice to the gods, so that they may look upon us with favour," Laertes reminded him, overcome with joy and sudden happiness. "But my Sicilian housekeeper must first make ready a bath and my best clothes. No more must I wear this tattered cloak as a sign of mourning!"

Afterwards, as Laertes, bathed and rubbed with fragrant oil, was leaving the bath, Pallas Athene appeared before him and with her divine power restored the sprightliness to his muscles and the beauty to his face.

He entered the parlour, and they all gazed in wonder at the transformation which had taken place. It seemed to them as if some divine creature had appeared among them.

Odysseus and Telemachus bowed low as a sign of their respect for him. The herdsmen who had accompanied Odysseus, and Laertes' servants, who were also invited to the feast, kissed his hand in veneration.

Then they took him to his seat at the head of the table, so that he might eat the first

mouthful of the fragrant roast meat, and drink the first draught of the sparkling wine.

Laertes raised his cup and said:

"I am only sorry, Odysseus, that I was not able to be in the palace yesterday, to stand at your side! I should dearly have liked to settle scores with those shameless philanderers."

Odysseus, too, raised his cup, and to drive out the regret which was creeping into his father's mind, cried:

"Why should you, father, worry over such things as that! We must no longer think of what has been, but rather be joyful for what the gods have granted us at this moment! May we remain in their favour; may all grief be at an end, just as my wanderings have finally ended!"

And with the noise of laughter and high spirits the feast began, and it was a feast worthy of a glorious king.

The Final Battle

But afterwards it seemed that there would be no end to enmity, wrath and hatred on Ithaca.

While Odysseus was rejoicing at meeting his father again in the orchard of his country home, the rumour of the fearful vengeance wrought on Penelope's suitors spread like wildfire. The fathers, sons and brothers of the dead were beginning to gather at the royal palace. They wept for their loved ones, carried them away and buried them, and amidst their tears and wailing began to plan *their* revenge.

And as Odysseus was revealing to his father who he was, and leading him to the celebration, the avengers of the dead were gathering in the meeting-place to listen as Eupeithes, father of the insolent Antinous, urged them to make bloody retaliation.

"Odysseus has committed terrible crimes," he ranted, sobbing with anger, "and he must answer to us for them! Let us rise against him at once, before he escapes our wrath, or we shall for ever be ashamed that we did not avenge the death of our sons and brothers. We will spare no one, friends! Forward!"

The blood ran to his head. He stood on

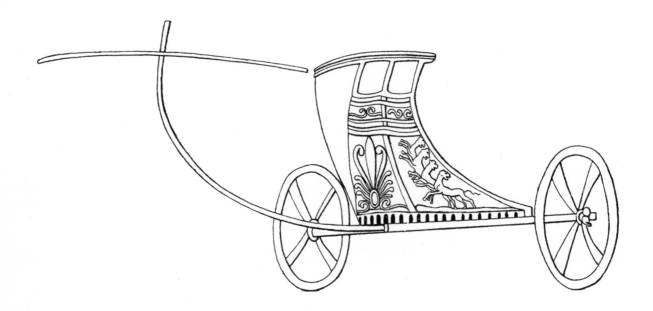

the platform, sword in hand and legs apart, and pointed with his blade to Odysseus' palace.

The metal points of spears glistened in the sun, and shields thudded darkly as men bent on vengeance struck them with the flat of their swords.

Another unrelenting battle was at hand. And it was in vain that Medon tried to speak reason to them:

"Ithacans, come to your senses! This thing has not happened without the will of the immortal gods! I saw with my own eyes how one of them assisted Odysseus, striking terror into his adversaries. He seemed to direct Odysseus' shots, which struck down one after the other those who mocked him and laid waste his palace!"

Old Halitherses, too, who had once warned Penelope's suitors, when the flight of an eagle revealed to him that the Ithacan king would return and punish them all, now raised a warning voice again:

"You brought this fearful destruction on yourselves! How many times have I warned you to watch over your sons better! How many times did I tell them to stop their crazy behaviour! How often did I tell them not to shame the unprotected Penelope, and not to strip bare Odysseus' house! It was no use — nothing was sacred to them. They said Odysseus would never return, that they might do as they pleased. They turned his palace into their lair, and you have seen the consequences for yourselves. And again I warn you: do not undertake any campaign

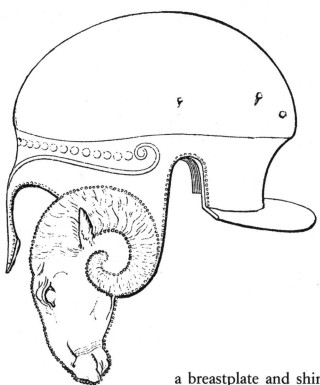

a breastplate and shin-guards, and was now picking up his bow and setting an arrow in place.

Beside him stood Telemachus, holding a sword and looking at his father as if to say: "Have no fear, father, that I should not give a good account of myself in battle! I will do no dishonour to our house, but will show my courage to the full!"

And on the other side of Odysseus was Laertes himself, with a glint in his eye, young and reborn, holding a lance in his

of vengeance against Odysseus! Or you will meet a similar fate!"

Some of the assembled noblemen were disconcerted by Halitherses' words, but others continued with their mindless thirst for blood. Their hands already on the hilts of their swords.

Soon they were grouping together and forming ranks. They hurried, filled with anger and hatred, towards Odysseus' palace.

Antinous' father, Eupeithes, the one whose life Odysseus had once saved, was at their fore, and again and again stirred up their passions with loud exhortations.

Outside the palace gates the crowd halted. They saw before them Odysseus, who had returned from his father's house; he wore

hand. Behind them in a row stood Odysseus' faithful herdsmen, and Dolius, steward of Laertes' house, and his six stalwart sons.

Two groups of warriors, face to face.

From beneath frowning brows looks of hatred flew like sparks. There was the ominous silence which forebodes a savage battle, and then an ear-rending screech cut through the warrior bands.

Laertes had, with enormous strength lent by the goddess Pallas Athene, thrown his heavy lance, which struck the front of Eupeithes' helmet. The point went straight through the metal; lord Eupeithes fell with a crash that shook the ground, and his armour clanged loudly.

Odysseus and Telemachus hurled themselves forward. A bitter struggle began.

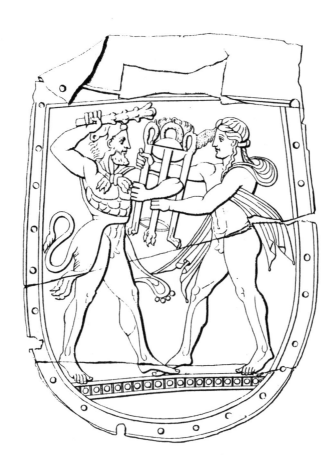

Reconciliation

Pallas Athene looked on the fight which was starting in front of Odysseus' palace with dissatisfaction.

The clash of arms, the ferocious shouts and the groans of the wounded reached Olympus itself, the home of the gods.

Could Odysseus even now, after such tribulations, after so many cruel struggles, not enjoy well-deserved peace at Penelope's side? Would retaliation follow retaliation for ever? And was blood to wash away blood till the end of human time?

The favourite daughter of Zeus, wise and prudent Pallas Athene, turned her clear gaze to the golden throne of Zeus, father of all gods and men.

"Lord of Olympus, father of us all; you can see what is happening down on Ithaca," she addressed him. "May I ask if it is your will that it should be so? Do you want the

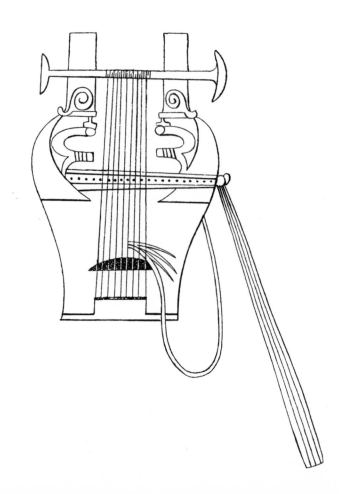

Greeks to stagger on in the fearful clamour of war, or would you prefer the two sides to be reconciled in friendship?"

Zeus turned a kind glance towards his best-loved daughter, from whom he never concealed anything, and whom he always obliged.

"Why do you ask me such things, child?" he said. "Was it not you who decided that Odysseus must return home to mete out just punishment for all the wrongs and evil deeds committed in his house? You must do as you think fit; I give you a free hand. Only I do not know what Poseidon will have to say, for he is still very angry with Odysseus. You know that he punished the Phaeacians for taking Odysseus safely to Ithaca; with one blow of his palm he turned their ship into a motionless, steep walled rock! So that

they might never again carry across the ocean those who are committed to his power! How great were the sacrifices they had to make to pacify him!"

"Poseidon, my dear father, will surely be appeased by Odysseus, too. He is already preparing a great sacrifice to him: a ram, a bull and a boar. I am sure your brother who rules all the seas with his trident will be satisfied."

"You are right, my child. We will arrange things so: Odysseus has punished the intruders in his house, all those arrogant suitors of his wife Penelope. May he reign in peace and contentment for many years. And so that no one might think of new revenge, I will wipe away from everyone's mind all recollection of the dead suitors. I do not wish to see more blood spilt!"

And to confirm his words he sent from his hand a smoking thunderbolt, which landed in the midst of the warring bands in front of Odysseus' palace.

"Thank you for your wise decision," Pallas Athene said, and in one bound she descended from Olympus to the Earth.

"Ithacans, stop fighting, spill no more blood!"

Zeus' lightning and the sonorous voice of Pallas Athene seemed to freeze all the commotion in an instant. Swords and lances fell onto the ground, and shields slipped from their arms.

The awe-stricken warriors saw Pallas Athene walk through their ranks and turn to Odysseus. They heard her say:

"Odysseus, clever and quick-witted son of Laertes: return your sword to its sheath and put aside your shield. There will be an end to all fighting, disputes and enmity! By the will of Zeus himself I come to make peace between you."

And as Odysseus' wise protectress had said it would be, so it was. Those who had run in fear from the field of battle returned, and no one raised a weapon in anger any more.

Peace was agreed; a funeral was held in memory of the dead, and as Tiresias had advised Odysseus when he visited the underworld, a ram, a bull and a boar were offered up to Poseidon.

Peace reigned on Ithaca.

The memory of wrongs suffered in the past was wiped from men's minds by the will of Zeus, as if it had been washed away by the waters of Lethe, the river of forgetfulness which flows through the underworld.

Many, many years passed in joy and contentment . . . They were quiet, and they were peaceful.

A farmer walks behind his team sowing seed; another digs over the soil around his fruit trees; up on the hillside in the sunshine a wine-grower ties back his vines, and a weaver beside her loom slips the shuttle through the warp.

One day after another passes in work, and year follows on from year. Clouds come and go; time digs lines in men's faces, makes their legs less steady, and takes the shine from their eyes.

In the palace of Ithaca, Laertes has long since died and Odysseus sits down on the silver couch inlaid with ivory, beside his faithful Penelope. He is very, very old. When he gently places his palm on the back of her hand, it shakes like a leaf floating to the ground in late autumn. Both have white hair now.

They often sit in front of the hearth and look into the flames, seeing there events which took place long ago, but which seem to the two of them as if they had happened yesterday . . .

And somewhere else, beside another hearth, an unknown blind singer reaches for his lute and begins to tell the tale of the bitter wanderings of Odysseus, and of his return to his beloved Penelope.

His name is Homer.

HOMER, THE ODYSSEY, AND ODYSSEUS

You have just read one of the most beautiful stories ever conjured up in a poet's mind.

It is also one of the oldest, since Homer lived sometime in the eighth century BC, which is a long, long time — nearly three thousand years — ago.

Homer, or Homeros, to give him his true name, belonged to the small nation of Greeks, living right at the tip of the Balkan Peninsula in south-eastern Europe. The ancestors of the modern Greeks, the ancient Greeks, were known as Hellenes, but Homer also calls them Achaeans.

They were a very enterprising people, brave, and endowed with both a keen intellect and sensitive feelings. At a time when most of the rest of Europe was covered in deep, unhospitable forest where herds of wild beasts roamed, and where most of the human inhabitants still lived a nomadic life, the Greeks had already built a highly cultured society. This was such a turning-point in history that we regard Greece as the "cradle" of European civilisation.

The soul of this remarkable nation was indeed stirred by restlessness and curiosity. The Greeks were interested in every aspect of both the world around them and the world within themselves.

Their systematic observation of their environment (this was the Greek's great innovation) laid the foundations of modern scientific thinking. They made the first real progress in astronomy, mathematics, geography, history, physics and, of course, philosophy.

Observation of the internal, spiritual life of man, on the other hand, gave rise to unique works of art — in sculpture, architecture and literature. The oldest forms of literary art seem to have been songs which were recited or sung to the accompaniment of a lute by wandering minstrels. We can imagine Homer himself as such a minstrel — perhaps Demodocus at the court of the Phaeacian king, Alcinous, described here in the Odyssey.

Since the Greeks were excellent seamen (and no less able merchants), they often came in contact with the nations inhabiting the shores of the Mediterranean, and on their journeys discovered and experienced many interesting things. They liked to tell tales of their travels when they returned to Greece and would use their lively imagination to enhance their stories. Originally independent stories somehow joined together with first one and then another tale, like beads on a string, and what were originally songs about a single adventure grew into a new poetic form, the epos, a long poem recounting the fates of heroes.

Both Homer's main works are epic poems: the Iliad, describing the siege of Troy by the

Greeks and their allies, and the Odyssey, recounting the many years' wanderings of the King of Ithaca on his way home from the Trojan War. Thus Homer did not invent either of the stories. The defeat of Troy and the adventures of Odysseus were certainly the subject of tales before Homer was born, perhaps long before. But he was the one who combined these well-known tales into a coherent and grandiose whole, reflecting the whole of the life and thought of his day.

We know from Homer how the ancient Greeks saw their gods, what very human qualities they attributed to them; from Homer we can get a picture of life at the courts of kings. He tells us what various objects, from weapons to warships, were like; he describes how the ancient Greeks dressed, how they ate, and the entertainments they enjoyed the most.

But more important still, the poet reveals to us the way of thinking and the emotions of his contemporaries. Here we are astonished to find how little they differed from people today. Their loves and hatreds, moments of bravery and of weakness, of joy and sadness, are like our own. Perhaps we see this most clearly of all in the account of the wanderings of the clever, and sometimes cunning, Odysseus.

The Iliad, where Odysseus was not the central figure, but merely one of the heroes of the war, concentrated on the quarrels between rulers, struggles for power and martial confrontation. The Odyssey, the younger of the two works, is, despite all the adventures and bitter fighting, rather different. Though Odysseus is a king, he longs for a peaceful life — he was even unwilling to join the Trojan expedition. His chief wish now that the hostilities have ended is to get back to his family and to bring back order to his homeland, which an arrogant and lazy aristocracy has begun to lay waste in his absence. Instead of a proud monarch, Homer depicts Odysseus as a caring father, who made his marital bed with his own hands and treats his subjects almost like members of the family. While the Iliad is a glorification of martial virtues, the Odyssey is the glorification of a desire for living in peace. In the Iliad the captains and warriors are depicted as the most important characters in the story, while in the Odyssey the poet's sympathies are clearly on the side of the peaceable rulers and the common people. Note how figures such as the herdsman Eumaeus, or the self-sacrificing servant Eurycleia, are sympathetically portrayed. All this brings Homer's poem and its heroes closer to the hearts of today's readers — as, for instance, does the unfaltering struggle of the heroic Odysseus for his right to a happy life. No wonder this figure has attracted the attention of writers and poets long after Homer, that they retell the story of Odysseus, seeing in it a reflection of the fate of modern man, who so often wanders from island to island, from one hope to another, from one obstacle to the next, like Homer's hero did.

Homer's hero? Was he really Homer's? For the person and life of this ancient poet are still shrouded in unsolved mysteries. We do not have the original verses of his two great works, only a later transcription from the reign of Pisistratus of Athens (6th century BC); we do not know whether Homer really was blind, as tradition would have it, or even when and where he was born. Since ancient times at least seven different places have vied for the honour of being acknowledged as his birthplace: the best-known of them include Athens and

Smyrna, although recent research suggests that it was the island of Chios off the coast of Turkey.

You do not need to know who Homer was to enjoy the Odyssey*: this beautiful tale of the long journey of the Ithacan king to restore good fortune to his homeland — a tale which conveys a message of hope to us, hope that perseverance, courage and fidelity to his ideals may in the end make a man master of his own fate, despite all the pitfalls and obstacles which beset him on the way. This is the immortal legacy of the poem, the reason Homer's* Odyssey *lives on as one of the greatest works of poetry ever written and ever to be written — it is a story you will want to read again and again.*

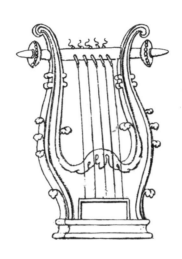

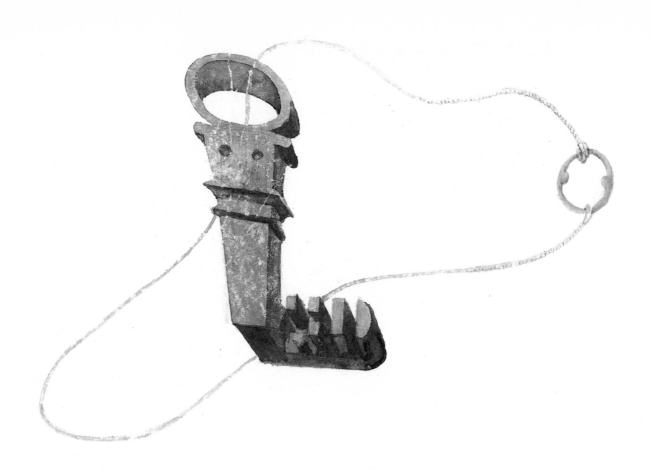

SOME CHARACTERS AND PLACES
FROM THE STORY

Achilles

The most famous of all the Greek heroes, he was one of the central figures in Agamemnon's army. He fought on the Trojan battlefield for nine years, conquering many of the neighbouring cities. Whenever he appeared among his enemies, he inspired terror and panic. In the tenth year of the war a dispute broke out between him and the commander-in-chief, Agamemnon (described by Homer in his *Iliad*), jeopardising the success of the entire venture. Without Achilles the Greeks found themselves on the brink of defeat, and were saved only because Achilles lent his famous armour to his best friend Patroclus, after the latter pleaded with him. At first the Trojans thought that Achilles had rejoined the battle, and they retreated. But they soon saw through the ruse, and Patroclus in his borrowed armour was slain by the Trojan prince Hector. The tragic death of his best friend so affected Achilles that he did indeed do battle again, and in hand-to-hand combat with Hector he stabbed the Trojan with his lance. But Achilles was not destined to live to see the final victory of his countrymen. When he was a baby his mother, the sea-goddess Thetis, had bathed him in the river Styx in the underworld, to make him invulnerable. However, he could be wounded in the heel where she had held him in the water. It was just this spot which the Trojan Paris (with the help of the god Apollo, whom Achilles had offended) struck with his arrow. There was a great struggle between the Greeks and Trojans for the body of the famous warrior, who had slain a wild boar at the age of ten, could outrun a deer, heal wounds and play enchanting tunes on the lyre. In the end the Greeks recovered it. They mixed the ashes of Achilles and his friend Patroclus, and raised a huge tombstone to their eternal glory.

Aegisthus

Cousin of the Mycenaean king Agamemnon, leader of the Greek forces at Troy. Deliberately avoiding participation in the war himself, he took the opportunity offered by the king's long absence to usurp the throne, with the aid of Agamemnon's wife, Clytemnestra. He claimed a right to it, saying his father, the Mycenaean king Thyestes, had been slain by Agamemnon in their struggle for power. But Thyestes himself had the death of Agamemnon's father Atreus on his conscience. Aegisthus ruled in Mycenae for another seven years after the murder of Agamemnon. In the eighth year Agamemnon's son Orestes avenged his father's death, killing Aegisthus and Clytemnestra. These mythical struggles for the throne of Mycenae have often been the subject of works of literature, including those by the famous dramatists Aeschylus, Euripides and Sophocles.

Aeneas

Son of the goddess Aphrodite and Anchises, of the Trojan royal family. On his father's suggestion he went with a strong force of armed men to the assistance of King Priam, and excelled by his heroic deeds during the Trojan war. After Hector he was the most feared and most fearless of the Greeks' enemies. He was the only one of the Trojan leaders to escape from the burning city after its defeat, taking with him his father and his small son Ascanius. This was the will of the gods, for Zeus himself had determined that Aeneas should find a new home in the west, in today's Italy. But it was only after several years' wandering and at the end of many adventures and bloody battles that Aeneas reached his new home, where he founded the Roman nation. The story is told in the epic poem the *Aeneid* by the Roman writer Virgil. It celebrates Aeneas as the father of the Romans and the epitome of Roman virtues.

Aeolus

Ruler of the winds, breezes, gales and storms, he lived on the Aeolian Isles in a splendid castle together with his six sons and six daughters. He spent the whole day feasting and merry-making while he watched over the four great winds. He kept the winds in caves and had the power to unleash, restrain or tame them. The west wind, who brought rain, was called *Zephyrus*, and was considered the protector of plant life. He was born in Aeolus' garden, which was why he was usually gentle, though he could also rant and rage (sometimes against the will of his master); then he would shriek terribly and bring violent storms. The south-west wind was called *Notus*; he brought with him heavy rain and was considered dangerous when he met his northern brother *Boreas*. Wild Boreas came from Thrace, and liked to wander the whole world. He was violent, icy, the origin of storms and blizzards. Much kinder was *Eurus*, the south-east wind, a mild and seldom dangerous fellow, often accompanied by refreshing rain.

Agamemnon

King of the rich kingdom of Mycenae, one of the most powerful of the rulers of mythical Greece. He was born in Mycenae, like his younger brother Menelaus, but came to the throne following years of exile in Sparta only after a bloody struggle in which he slew his uncle Thyestes. When Menelaus married the stepdaughter of the King of Sparta, Helen, Agamemnon married her half-sister Clytemnestra. They had four children, a son, Orestes, and three daughters, of whom Iphigenia met the cruellest fate. Agamemnon led the Greek armies to Troy and to ensure their success he was ready to sacrifice Iphigenia to the gods. At the siege of Troy Agamemnon had a dispute with the famous Greek warrior, Achilles, which almost brought about the failure of the whole

expedition. After the fall of Troy Agamemnon returned to his native Mycenae with rich booty, but in the ten years he had been away his cousin Aegisthus had seized power in the city. With help from Clytemnestra he had Agamemnon killed at supper, like, as Homer puts it, "a bull at the trough".

Ajax

Son of King Telamon of Salamis, one of the boldest of the Greek warriors. It was due largely to his valour that the body of Achilles was prevented from falling into the hands of the Trojans. After an heroic struggle, in which he was assisted by Odysseus, he snatched the body from the enemy and brought it back to the

Greek camp to receive full funeral honours. But a quarrel broke out between him and Odysseus as to who should get the great Greek warrior's magnificent armour, which the hero's mother had said should go to whoever played the greatest role in recovering her son's body. Each of them was convinced that he deserved the armour. In the end the dispute was won by Odysseus, and Ajax, who considered it a terrible disgrace, killed himself with his own sword; Ajax remained an irreconcilable enemy of Odysseus even in the underworld.

Alcmene

One of the spirits Odysseus saw in the underworld, she was the founder of the Mycenaean royal house, and mother of the famous Greek hero, Heracles. His father was none other than Zeus himself, and so after his death Heracles was raised up to Olympus to join the gods.

Aphrodite

The most beautiful of all the Greek goddesses, goddess of beauty and love. She received from Paris (son of Priam, the King of Troy) the golden apple from the Garden of the Hesperides, which was inscribed *"for the most beautiful"*. It was due to her great beauty that she became one of the most powerful and most worshipped of the gods. Her favourite shrine was at Paphos, on the island of Cyprus, where there was a grove and an altar sacred to her. She wore a magnificent golden tiara and belt which had the magic power to arouse love and passion. As protectress of lovers she was assisted by a number of other deities, such as Charis, goddess of grace, Hymen, god of marriage, and Eros, god of love. Though she was goddess of love, she was not lucky in love herself. Nor did her favour help the Trojans in their struggle against the Greeks. Her intervention on behalf of the Cyprian sculptor Pygmalion was more successful — she brought to life one of his statues, a girl he had fallen in love with. And though Aphrodite herself was beauty incarnate, her husband was the ugliest of all the divinities, the lame, clumsy and ever-grimy Hephaestus, the god of craftsmen and fire.

Ariadne

Another of those Odysseus met in his descent to the underworld; she was the lovely daughter of the Cretan king, Minos. In the labyrinth of his palace, with its many halls and chambers and interwoven passages, there lived a monstrous bull, the Minotaur. To atone for deeds committed long ago the Athenians had to offer the Minotaur a cruel sacrifice every nine years — ten young men and ten maidens, which it would eat. At last the bold Athenian prince Theseus set out for Crete to stop this sacrifice and slay the monster. But he could not have succeeded without the aid of Ariadne, who fell in love with him and gave him a sword and a ball of thread with which to find his way out of the labyrinth. Ariadne was not, however, destined to become Theseus' wife. She was forced to marry the god Dionysus, but the match was an unhappy one, and Ariadne soon died of grief and of longing for Theseus.

Eos

Sister of the sun god Helios. Goddess of the dawn, she rose every morning from her bed in Oceanus and stepped into her shining chariot drawn by two pink horses, to bring mankind the light of a new day. The Greeks thought of her as a pretty girl who loved all that was beautiful, young and fresh, which is why she often took a fancy to graceful young men, whom she would simply carry off. One of these was Tithonus, son of the King of Troy Laomedon, with whom she

had two sons. The second of these, Memnon, was one of the most beautiful of mortals. During the Trojan war he assisted King Priam, and after the death of Hector even led the defence, until he himself fell in combat with Achilles.

Epicasta

Also known as Jocasta, she was among those Odysseus saw in Hades. Wife of the King of Thebes, Laius, her fate was an unpleasant one: she married a second time, unwittingly to her own son, Oedipus. When, after many years, she discovered the truth, she hanged herself in despair. Her story is told by many of the classical dramatists, the profoundest and most famous play being that of Sophocles.

Hades

The surly and ever gloomy god of the underworld, ruler of the realm of the dead; he and his brothers Zeus and Poseidon were the most powerful of all the gods. His kingdom was deep beneath the Earth, separated from the other gods and from men, and not a single ray of sunlight penetrated there. Its grim, desolate plain was bounded by five rivers: *Styx*, the river of hatred, *Acheron*, the river of grief, *Cocytus*, the river of wailing, *Lethe*, the river of forgetfulness,

● SOME CHARACTERS AND PLACES FROM THE STORY ●

Hector

If Achilles was the fiercest warrior of the Greeks, then Hector was the Trojans' champion fighter. He was the eldest son of King Priam and Queen Hecuba. Bravest and most noble of the Trojan warriors, it was chiefly because of him, as commander of the defending forces that the city was able to hold out for a full nine years against odds of two to one. When Hector heard that, following his quarrel with Agamemnon, Achilles had left the ranks of the Greek army, he counter-attacked and forced the Greeks to retreat. He killed Achilles' friend Patroclus in combat, and then challenged Achilles himself to a fight to the death. But after a bitter struggle he was killed. King Priam begged the victor for his body, so that he might have a funeral on the soil of his native Troy. After twelve days (during which time Achilles had promised to maintain a truce in honour of his great adversary) the Trojans mourned their hero, burnt his body on a funeral pyre, placed his ashes in a golden urn and raised a huge tombstone over it.

and *Phlegethon*, the river of flame. Somewhere in the darkest part of the underworld was Hades' golden palace, from where he ruled over his dismal realm with his wife Persephone. Hades and Persephone also ruled over a number of minor deities which filled people with fear, such as the Empusae, who waylaid travellers, Hypnus, god of deep, trance-like sleep, and the Erinyes, merciless goddesses of vengeance and guilt. The souls of the dead reached Hades by way of a number of dark abysses; one of the entrances to the underworld was in the west, beyond Oceanus, which is where Odysseus entered. He was one of the few living creatures — along with Heracles and Orpheus — to visit the place. Hades, though one of the gods, was avoided by most of them, who did not like him. People, in order to ingratiate themselves with him, would offer black sheep as sacrifices; he was also worshipped as the giver of riches from the bowels of the Earth.

Helios

He was the sun god and the most radiant of the Olympian gods. A tall figure with golden hair and a shining crown of light around his head, he left his magnificent palace on the banks of Oceanus every morning, riding in a golden chariot, and poured down brightness and warmth to the Earth below. Each evening he returned to his home after his day's travels. The god of sunshine was revered and loved by all earthly creatures (not only people but also animals), and by all of the gods on Olympus. Only Hades, who liked to live in eternal darkness, disliked him strongly. On the island of Thrinacie Helios had seven herds of cows and seven flocks of rams, each of fifty animals, which were watched over by two of his daughters. According to Greek legend the three hundred and fifty sacred cows represented the 350 days of the year, and the three hundred and fifty rams the 350 nights.

Hephaestus

Born to Zeus and Hera as an ugly cripple, he was rejected by his mother and thrown from Olympus into Oceanus. But there he was taken care of by the sea goddesses Eurynome and Thetis, who brought him up in their underwater cave and had him taught the blacksmith's trade. He soon mastered it to perfection, and worked for the Olympians (he built the golden palaces in which the gods dwelt). He made Achilles' famous armour and magnificent shield, and for King Menelaus he made the beautiful silver wine spoon the king gave to Telemachus (Odysseus'

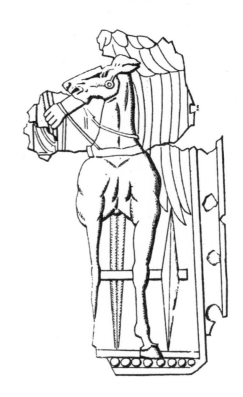

son). In order to pursue his beloved craft, Hephaestus built himself a large forge in a volcano, so that he might have plenty of fire at hand. He was the god of fire and blacksmiths, and nearly all other crafts, especially those in which fire was used. Homer says his wife was the beautiful Aphrodite, but other legends have it she was the goddess of beauty, Charis, though he himself was ugly, always sooty, and a little clumsy, so that the gods of Olympus would often make fun of him.

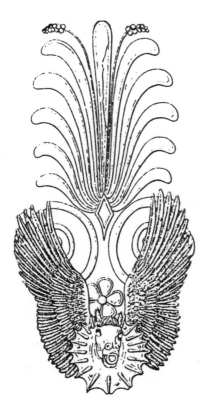

Hera

Greatest of the goddesses, queen of the heavens, she sat on her throne on Olympus beside her husband and brother, Zeus. He was enchanted by her beauty, especially her lovely eyes. Hera was an exemplary and dignified wife, and was the goddess of marriage and motherhood. She and Zeus sometimes quarrelled violently, usually because the lord of Olympus took a fancy to some other goddess, or even to some beautiful mortal. At such times there was, literally, a storm on Olympus, for the thunder, lightning and mists were under Hera's power and obeyed her will. She often took a hand in the affairs of men, and would argue with her husband over this. She and Zeus had two sons, Ares, god of war, and Hephaestus, armourer and blacksmith of the gods, and one daughter, the eternally young Hebe, whose task it was to see to the needs of the gods when feasts were held.

Hermes

He had the sometimes ungrateful task of carrying messages and instructions from Zeus, but he should be regarded more as a sort of experienced personal secretary. He was a skilful negotiator, ingenious to the point of being cunning, and did not worry too much over the odd unfulfilled promise or broken vow. The very day he was born he escaped from his cradle and invented the lyre from a tortoise shell, which he learnt to play within a few hours. He was just as quick in learning to speak, and on that first day of his life also managed to steal Apollo's herd of cows. Zeus was pleased with his son, and at once appointed him his personal envoy; he would send him out especially on complicated missions or where confidentiality was paramount. And Hermes fulfilled all his tasks with complete reliability. Apart from his job as an envoy he was also the patron of travellers, rhetoricians, merchants, sportsmen, inventors and physicians — and also of tricksters and thieves!

Jason

One of the best-known figures in Greek mythology, he commanded the huge *Argo*, a ship with fifty oars, in which he and his companions the Argonauts set out for distant Colchis. He wanted to bring back the golden fleece — the fleece of the golden-winged ram — which hung in the temple guarded by a dragon. Jason undertook the journey to win the throne of the kingdom of Iolcus from his half-brother, who had usurped it, and said he would only give up the throne if Jason accomplished this awesome task. Luckily, the goddess Hera said she would help him. During the voyage the *Argo* faced endless dangers, including the Symplegades Rocks crushing ships and their crew, and the Sirens whose beautiful songs lured men to their death. Here, too, Jason owed his success to Hera's intervention.

Leucothea

This Greek goddess was originally a mortal, daughter of King Cadmus, the founder of the famous Greek city of Thebes. Zeus gave her his son Dionysus, later the god of wine, to bring up; his mother was Leucothea's sister Semele, who died giving birth to him. Ino, as she was originally called, thus brought upon herself the wrath of Zeus' wife. The powerful Hera sent madness to Ino's husband, who in a fit of rage

killed one of their sons, and when he threatened the second, in desperation Ino threw herself into the sea with the child in her arms. Zeus later made her a goddess out of gratitude for bringing up Dionysus, and her son was also turned into a sea god. Under her new name of Leucothea she became the protectress of sailors and drowning men, and patron of a calm sea.

Menelaus

Agamemnon's brother and son of the Mycenaean king Atreus, he ruled in Sparta as the successor to King Tyndareus. He acquired the throne by marrying Tyndareus' daughter Helen. But she was only the king's stepdaughter, since her real father was Zeus. After the fall of Troy Menelaus returned home to his kingdom only after eight years' wandering, via Lesbos, Egypt, Libya and Phoenicia, and the mouth of the River Nile, where the sea god Proteus told him how to appease the gods so that they might allow him to return home. While visiting the King of Egypt he was given a drink which caused forgetfulness of all evils and defeats past. He and Helen drank it, and thus both forgot the unfortunate past: Menelaus forgot his wanderings, Helen forgot that she had left her husband to run away with Paris. As a recompense for all the sufferings they had had during their lifetime the gods brought them after their death to Elysium, the blissful land without cares or woes.

Nestor

The oldest, most just and most prudent of the Greek leaders at Troy, which is why Telemachus went to him to ask advice when he decided to try to find his father, Odysseus. He was respected and honoured throughout Greece, and reigned in Pylos for many decades — when he joined Agamemnon's expedition to Troy he was already ruling a third generation of his subjects. He acquired fame in his youth with many brave deeds, and at Troy, too, he excelled in battle against many younger adversaries. He was the only one of the Greek rulers to try to settle the dispute between Agamemnon and Achilles. He returned from the war unscathed, but was saved from certain death there by his son Antilochus,

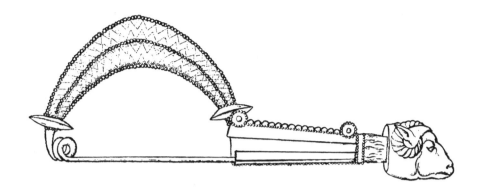

who caught in his own body a spear thrown at Nestor by the chief ally of the Trojans, the warrior king Memnon.

Oceanus

This was not an ocean, or a sea, but a huge river flowing round the Earth. It was the origin of all the rivers and seas, including the rivers of Hades; and the sun, moon and stars rose from it and set in it — except for the Great Bear constellation. Oceanus was an extremely powerful god, born of the god of the heavens, Uranus, and the mother of Earth, Ge; he was therefore the brother of Zeus' father Cronus, and one of the oldest of the Greek deities. He was sometimes considered the origin of the whole Universe, perhaps because of

his extreme fertility: with his wife and sister Tethys he had no less than three thousand sons and three thousand daughters.

Olympus

The highest mountain in Greece, on the borders of Thessaly and Macedonia; about 3000 m (9,800 ft) high. It was the home of the gods, who lived there in golden palaces built by Hephaestus, in eternal bliss, leisure and entertainment. They were immortal, eternally youthful, and taller and more beautiful than mortals, although they had many human traits. Unlike the grim underworld home of Hades or the cave palace of Poseidon, Olympus was a place of eternal light. The twelve major gods and other minor deities met there at Zeus' golden throne, which was also the work of Hephaestus. He built Hera an exquisite bedchamber with a secret lock which only she could open, and for himself he made a magnificently equipped forge, also of pure gold. During their almost incessant feasting, the gods were served the divine drink, nectar, and the divine food, ambrosia, by the goddess of youth, Hebe, and the beautiful Trojan prince Ganymede, who was carried there by an eagle on orders from Zeus himself. This heavenly diet assured eternal youth. The ancient Greeks imagined Olympus to be of immense height — when Zeus once became enraged with

Hephaestus and hurled him down from the mountain, he flew a full nine days before striking the ground on the island of Lemnos.

Pallas Athene

Most beloved daughter of the ruler of the gods, Zeus. Legend had it she was born without a mother direct from Zeus' head — from which she leapt in full armour! She was his favourite, and he concealed nothing from her, often confided in her, and never, it would seem, denied her requests. Athene also worshipped her father, even declining to marry though she was beautiful and keen-witted. She was the goddess of just and prudent war and of wisdom, and patroness of the arts and artistic crafts (she was said to teach women weaving and men the goldsmith's craft and building). She took a hand in natural events (calming the sea, holding back the dawn), and also in the affairs of mankind, appearing to humans in many different guises. The Ithacan king Odysseus was a major protégé of hers. She assisted him from the very start of the Trojan war when she took her revenge on Paris, and subsequently on his return journey and in the struggle with Penelope's suitors. Next to Zeus she was the most powerful of the Olympians, and among the Greeks, she was the most honoured.

Patroclus

One of the greatest heroes of Agamemnon's hundred-thousand strong army, the closest friend of Achilles, he was honourable, straightforward, courageous and faithful. When in the tenth year of the siege of Troy Achilles argued with Agamemnon and refused to fight, on the suggestion of Nestor Patroclus begged his friend to lend him his armour and in it faced

Hector, commander of the Trojan forces. He was killed in the combat, and his death led Achilles to resume fighting in order to avenge his friend's death.

Persephone

In the gloom of the underworld kingdom Persephone was the cruel and merciless queen of Hades, though she became his wife against her will. Hades abducted her as a young girl and made her his wife, despite protests to Zeus by her mother Demeter. In the end it was decided

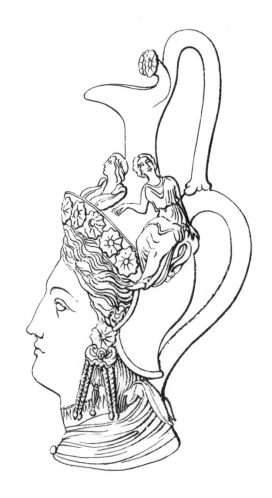

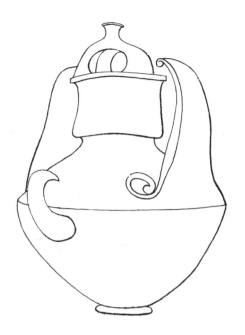

Phorcys

The bay in the south of Ithaca where the Phaeacians brought Odysseus to safety was named after the sea-god Phorcys. Phorcys, also called The Old Man of the Sea, was in charge of all the monsters of the deep. By his wife Ceto he fathered a number of them himself, including the Gorgon, with snakes for hair, of which Odysseus was so afraid in the underworld, and the dragon Ladon, keeper of the golden apples in the garden of the Hesperides. It was here that the apple came from which Paris (son of the King of Troy) gave as the prize in the contest between the goddesses Hera, Pallas Athene and Aphrodite, with the inscription *"for the most beautiful"*.

that she would remain Hades' wife, but would return to Earth every year for a certain period. So every spring Persephone went back to her mother Demeter, goddess of the harvest, who at that time of year gave plants the power of germination so she could welcome her daughter with flowers and greenery, until in autumn she left again for the underground kingdom of darkness.

Poseidon

Ruler of the sea and all its lesser gods and goddesses; together with his brothers Zeus and Hades overthrew their father Cronus and divided the sovereignty of the world between them. Poseidon became the ruler of all matters concerning the sea. He lived in a fine palace near Aegae from where he would ride out over the surface of the sea, which parted in front of his golden chariot, drawn by horses with golden manes. He was armed with a large trident, with which he could strike the ground to bring on earthquakes. He had a fickle, cantankerous and irritable nature, and quarrelled with the other gods almost daily. Once he even took part in an unsuccessful revolt against the authority of Zeus. He was worshipped mainly by sailors, and his favourite sacrifice was a ram and a bull. Poseidon's offspring were numerous, both the one-eyed giant Polyphemus and the god Proteus numbering among his sons, as well as Triton, the marine messenger, who was half man, half fish.

Tiresias

A famous blind seer from Thebes who had great prophetic powers. On his return journey from Troy Odysseus went to Hades to ask him what awaited him and his companions on the journey back to Ithaca — the great man's wisdom lasted not only throughout his exceptionally long life on Earth (he is said to have outlived seven generations) but also in the underworld after his death. Some legends say Tiresias received the gift of prophesy from Zeus, but according to others it was from Pallas Athene. As well as seeing the future, Tiresias was able to understand the language of birds.

Zeus

Mightiest ruler of gods and men, he lived on Olympus in a magnificent and luxurious palace built for him by his son Hephaestus. This most majestic, most powerful and wisest of the gods had, however, to fight hard for his supremacy. Briefly, he gained it after rebelling against his father, the god Cronus. In a bitter struggle lasting ten years he and his brothers Hades and Poseidon overthrew Cronus and then divided sovereignty over the world among themselves. Zeus, the youngest, received heaven and Earth, while the middle brother Poseidon became ruler

Proteus

Both son and servant of Poseidon, he lived near the island of Pharos, where Poseidon's wife Amphitrite kept fish and seals. Apart from an intimate knowledge of the depths of the sea, he had the gift of prophesy, but was most unwilling to reveal the future to anyone. To escape those who wanted to ask him questions, he would constantly alter his shape, for example by changing into a sea creature, then into a wild beast, and then into a river.

● SOME CHARACTERS AND PLACES FROM THE STORY ●

246

of the sea, and Hades, the eldest, of the underworld. As the supreme deity, Zeus was above all the lord of nature: he showed his power with thunder and lightning, which he hurled down from Olympus whenever he was seized by rage or something was not to his liking. He often took action not only against mortals, but also against the inferior gods. He was the protector of law and order, of travellers, and of beggars, and he saw to it that promises and oaths were kept. He sent good or evil to men, and it was through him that they accumulated wealth, but also by his will that they lost their senses, fell into poverty, or escaped from it. Zeus was the supreme and the most powerful god but he had many human qualities: he could be bad-tempered, tired, envious, rash. He would rest from his exertions in ruling the world at his favourite haunts (such as Mount Ida in Crete), but he liked above all to be on Olympus, where he held rich banquets. At these the head waiter, the beautiful youth Ganymede, served nectar, the divine drink, and ambrosia, food of the gods, while Hebe, goddess of youth and a daughter of Zeus, entertained the mightiest of the gods with song and dance. By his side sat his wife Hera, a stately goddess with whom in the course of their stormy marriage he had three children. The Greeks had many names for him, such as almighty, thundering, all-seeing, cloud-gathering, or simply father of gods and men, as Pallas Athene, his best-loved daughter, would call him. And they imagined him as a venerable, elderly man with a long beard and an expression full of the dignity of a mighty ruler.

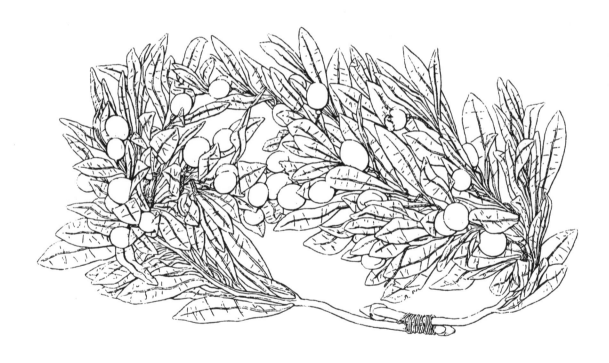

● SOME CHARACTERS AND PLACES FROM THE STORY ●